DISTANT
DRUMS

David L. Weeks
"Ancient Tradition"

Introduction
R. Jalani Horton
HouseOfBambu

CONQUERING LION ENTERPRISE

Published & Marketed by
CONQUERING LION ENTERPRISE
St. Croix, Virgin Islands

Contact: facebook.com/AncientTradition

Copyright © 2021 by David L. Weeks
Cover Design by Wes Richards

All poems were written by David L. Weeks, except where noted.
When necessary, some individuals' names and details have been
changed to maintain anonymity and respect privacy.

Discretion Advised. Some parts of this book deal with subjects that
are intended for mature audiences only.

ISBN-13: 978-0-9701711-3-9

Manufactured in The United States of America

There Is Nothing New Under JAH Sun,
But Everyone Has A Unique Testimony!

To lala,
It is a pleasure
meeting you, I appreciate
your support.

Love,

Daviid

This book is "Livicated" to the living memory of my Father, Egbert L. Weeks, & my Mother, Sarah V. Weeks; I carry you in My Heart!

To my first best friend, Dave Benta, rest in your own unique way, Brother!

Thank you to EVERYONE who has supported me throughout the years in all my endeavors.

A Very Special Thanks to Wesley Richards, Jalani Horton, Cleo Christian, Raymond Abramson, Randy Abramson

All Thanks and Praises to THE MOST HIGH, JAH RASTAFARI, for the gift of Creativity and for HIS Inspiration.

PREFACE

Early in my writing career, I was once asked if I ever worry about writer's block. My response was, "No...if I never write another poem, it just means I have said all that I had to say." This book represents the height of a journey of writing poetry, or *messages*—as I used to call them. This does not necessarily mean I have nothing left to say. Let's just propose; I have said all that I had to say in this literary medium. There just might be more to come.

The book's canon begins with **Throwback.** I return to my roots and pay homage to my beginnings, with a diverse assembly of my earliest writings. For one reason or another, these poems never made it into my first book.

I Am African is an honorable "head nod" to my big brother, Dean L. Weeks. The chapter features a collection of his original poems.

Some poems just refuse to be categorized. **Don't Put Me In A Box** is where I had to place these renegade "Free Verse." They are not love lyrics, nor are they on any type of spiritual or righteous trip. Each of these poems has its own energy and vibe.

Give The People What They Want is a collection of commissioned pieces written for a special occasion or for someone special.

Intimacy is much more than primal instincts. As human beings, we must exist on a higher plane. **Bring Me A Higher Love** is all about that spiritual love.

Word Sound, Power! Within the RastafarI way of life is the precept: Word, Sound, and Power. Every word has a sound, and every sound has a vibration; this vibration can be positive or negative. To put it in a complete thought for you to Overstand. The Sound of Words has the Power to influence, positively or negatively. My hope is that the words in this chapter and throughout this book will positively impact you.

I-Rose: My Fire Angel. This chapter is Livicated to My First Lover. No woman has ever loved me the way She did, and no woman ever will!

What's Love Got To Do With It? These poems fall somewhere between that higher love and carnal pleasure. Sometimes love has everything to do with what we are feeling; sometimes it doesn't!

Rudeness Or Human Nature? This chapter is for mature readers. Yes, these erotic poems are for entertainment…but the chapter's title delves into aspects of an age-old controversial debate. Do these amorous musings belong outside of the bedroom, in a book, for theater, or…not?

She Said He Said. In my writing journey, I have had the honor of collaborating on numerous compositions (duets) with remarkable poets. I have always enjoyed the creative challenge and freestyle nature of such partnerships…improvising as we flow in and out of each other's verses. They write a verse, then I write a verse; I write a verse, then they…

A solemn tribute to the peaceful end of a relationship. **Season's End**

I Wrote A Song are lyrics that I wrote with a melody in my head.

In African culture and tradition, one of the ancient functions of The *Drums* was to send *messages*, sometimes across great *Distances*. In the modern western way of life, "drumming is, most often, about entertainment." Yet, drums still hold profound, spiritual, and venerable importance in the African way of life—on the continent and the diaspora. It is within this *Ancient Tradition* that I present this book of *Messages* to you. Distant Drums!

David L. Weeks
"Ancient Tradition"
2021

TABLE OF CONTENTS

INTRODUCTION

This book opens and ends with "Distant Drums." From the beginning, David sets the reader on a path, a curvaceous, color-filled, and testified landscape, that brings the reader back different. Yes, "different!" The Drums you hear in the beginning strike differently in the end. This is a beautiful, passionate, courageous journey.

To return "different," one must simply be open to creating space in one's mind and spirit to feel. Like the best writers, David forces you to create that space in a way that you will be laughing, smiling, and reflecting. You will experience comfort and discomfort, but most certainly, you will feel. This is not airy-fairy poetry; this is not deep-deep worldly revelations either. This is a "unique" testimony from "Fiya Mammie's" glowing Sun, who "sometimes roar."

I was surprised how far "Distant Drums" reached into my own experiences. It made me reflect on mistakes, on achievements, on moments where the world stood still in joy and pure bliss. I was open to feel or see wherever it took me, and it was a joy—an absolutely great experience for any reader willing to take a walk.

Some poems and expressions, throughout the book, made me pick up my pen and jot down ideas, phrases, and words. They were inspirational, stimulating, and profound throughout…great perspectives and points of view. Poems like "Lasana" and "Jazz;" and "My Road" struck me more and more. Raw, alive, emotive, and gracious.

This book of poetry is a literary gem, a ride-or-die-like partner. It fits in the many small spaces that we call life, and I wonder. Why is David so able to commit these feelings to ink? Why are his words so real, and why does the fabric of his words feel so comfortable? I figure it's from his "un-orthodox walk" or his "blurred speech." Natural reasons for heightened awareness and sensibilities that some remarkable persons share. You be the judge.

David shares his humanity with the Universe, and we are all made better for it. It is courageous and educational, liberating and entertaining...all at the same time. I can imagine a short movie, a script based on the landscapes David has drawn for me, the reader. I see my experiences, feelings, and face in his poems, but his words have their own unique testimony. What a joy!

I can hear and feel the "Distant Drums."

R. Jalani Horton
Father, Lover, Bredren & Dreamer
HouseOfBambu

CHAPTER I
THROWBACK

DISTANT DRUMS

I Hear The Sound Of The Drums
Riding On The Wind
Sounding From Mount Zion
The Drums!
The Distant Drums, The Beating Drums
Beating, Sending, Sending A Message
"Africa, Africa, Africa Unite!
Get Up, Stand Up
Stand Up For Your Rights!"
Drums Beating For Freedom
Beating For Liberation
Beating For Unity
Black Freedom, Black Liberation, Black Unity
The Drums!

Distant Drums, Ancient Drums
Telling My-Story, My Black-Story
Djembe, Udu, The Talking Drums
Talking About Imhotep
Hannibal, Akhenaton, Makeda,
Pianky, Cleopatra
Talking About Zenobia, Nzinga,
Chaka, Chaka Zulu, Menelik I
The Drums!
Drums Sounding From The Bottom
Of The Deep
Speaking The Names Of Billions Of Africans
Who Died, On Slave Ships
On The Journey Into Slavery
Drums, Sounding From The Bowels
Of The Earth
Speaking The Names Of Africans
Who Died, On Big Plantations.
The Drums!

17

The Sound Of The Drums
The Distant Drums
Rides On The Ocean Waves
From Across The Atlantic
Sounding From The Land Of My Forefathers
Alke-Bu-Land, The Black Land
Distant Drums
Sounding From Across The Harbor
Sounding The Call Of The Black Star Liner
Ready For Departure
Sounding The Call
Repatriation, Repatriation
The Drums!
The Calling Drums, Calling
Calling You, Calling Me
Calling, I n I
Calling RastafarI.
The Drums!

I Hear The Distant Drums
Of The Prophets Of Old
The Drums Of Isaiah:
"Woe Unto Them That Call Evil Good,
And Good Evil; That Put Darkness For
Light, And Light For Darkness; That Put
Bitter For Sweet, And Sweet For Bitter."
The Drums Of Ezekiel:
"Thus Saith THE LORD; Behold,
I Will Take The Children Of Israel
From Among The Heathen, Whither They
Be Gone, And Will Gather Them On
Every Site, And Bring Them Into
Their Own Land."
The Drums!

Yes, I Hear The Distant Drums
Chanting Drums, The Bass Drums

The Akette, The Fundi Drums
Niyabingi Drums.
I Hear Niyabingi Drums
Chanting!
Chanting, Babylon Your Throne Gone Down
Babylon Your Throne Gone Down
Drums Beating For Over 400 Years
By The Rivers Of Babylon, Drums That Will
Never Stop Beating, Until Babylon Walls Burn Down.
The Drums!

Listen, And You Will Hear The Drums
The Distant Drums Of Life, The Distant
Drums Of Creation.
In The Beginning, Was The Drums
And The Drums Were With JAH
And JAH Played The Drums
And JAH Chanted, And Whatsoever JAH Chanted,
Sounded Irie. The Drums!

1989 NEWS FLASH

Everywhere you looked, the walls of bondage
Were coming down;
Yet South Afrika is still not free.
Well, I guess We have the right to tumble
Ours down.

Just this past year, Mr. president made
A couple of decisions; he gave China a break,
And Panama he invaded.
Contradiction, Contradiction. As I said before,
Mr. President, he makes all the right
Decisions.

South Afrika crowned a new President.
Russia's beginning to tame the "big bear."

The Nation of Islam is back,
Mosque Mariam was livicated in February.
Farrakhan takes a stand for Black People
And says, "Stop The Killing."
As-Salaam Alaikum.

BLACK TO BLACK

Never lose sight Black Man
Of the Beauty in Me. That True
Beauty that comes from within Me,
Enhances the beauty without Me.

Look to Me Black Man, for the
Heaven You seek is within Me.
The Savior You await will not fall
From the sky, He will come from Me.

Set Your Eyes on Me Black Man and
Share Your Love with Me. The secrets
Of My heart and womb are what I share
Of Me.

Never lose sight Black Woman
Of the strength in Me. That strong
Spirit that's within Me gives Me
My stone-hard physique.

Look to Me Black Woman, for the
Kingdom You seek is within Me.
The generation of Righteous Warriors
Will come from Me.

Set Your Eyes on Me Black Woman and
Share Your Love with Me. The secrets
Of My heart and testicles are what I share
Of Me.

One Love

LA BORIQUA

Una hermosa mujer negra
Con un suave sabor latino
Salsa picante caliente
Con un toque afrikano

Su espíritu muestra
A través de su sonrisa
Amor compasivo
Y sensibilidad
Estos son los principios
De su corazón

Me imagino
Bailando al ritmo
De su caminar
Cuando sus caderas ruedan
Escucho tambores afrikanos
Escucho un ritmo seductor

Ella es una mujer
Para todas las estaciones
Me calienta
En invierno frío
Noches
Me enfría
En el caliente
Calor de verano

Ella es como
Una brisa fresca
En un claro
Día primaveral
Como un chile
En el aire
En un crujiente

22

Noche de otoño

Su toque
Como chispas ...
.... Enciende el fuego
De amor

ELEGANCE

There's just something about you
About the way you move
Like The lyrics to my song
Your Body Flows

The way you walk
The way your hips roll
The way you stand
It's just Vogue

A body soft and smooth
Curved to perfection, mm mm mm
A style
Unique and true
You wear the clothes
The clothes do not wear you

Soul filling essence
A radiant aura strong and bold
There is no doubt
Who's gracing the floor
No doubt
Who's strutting the runway
A presence with an attitude
Commands the audience
All eyes are fixed on you

Lips, sensuous and full
Eyes soft and mellow
Face inviting
Always adorned
With a seductive look

Elegant Is What You Are!

FIRE IN MY EYES

Billion of Afrikans died in The Middle Passage
Billions of Afrikans died for the establishment of colonialism
Billions of Afrikans died because they refused to compromise who
they Were

Robbed of our Motherland
Robbed of our Afrikan Names
Robbed of our Afrikan Culture
Robbed of our Afrikan-story
Robbed of our Afrikan Religion
Robbed of our GOD

Black Postmaster lynched, and his wife and four daughters shot
and maimed,
Lake City. SC., 1968
Emmett Till murdered for whistling at a white woman, 1955
Four Black girls killed in the bombing of a church, Birmingham,
Alabama, 1964
Malcolm X assassinated, 1965
Martin Luther King, Jr. assassinated, 1968
Blacks Massacred in Orangeburg, SC. 1968

Hundreds of Afrikans murdered in South Afrika
Hundreds of Young Afrikans massacred in Sharpeville
Hundreds of Young Afrikans massacred in Soweto
Stephen Biko died in chains
Yusef Hawkins murdered...
...
Yet, some still ask,
Why do some of us show anger towards the whiteman?
Why are some of us vengeful towards the whiteman?
Why are some of us non-compromising, non-apologetic, and
Non-sympathetic when it comes to the whiteman.

Why is there Fire In My Eyes? Niyabingi!

FRIENDS OR LOVERS

Where Do Lonely Hearts Go,
Do They Find Each Other?
Or do they continue their
Separate way...
Never getting together,
Never exploring The Love
Of Each Other.

We have been friends
For such a long time,
And tonight is just another
Ordinary night.
I have been next to you many
Many times, but I've never felt
Such a feeling like this before.

There must be something mystic
In the air, 'cause I Feel It,
And I want To know,
Do You Feel It Too? Something is
Putting Me in a Romantic mood,
And for some reason,
I want to get Romantic with You.

Will this put our Friendship in jeopardy,
Is this the beginning of a sticky situation,
Or is this a Natural thing, destined to happen?
We should get together, test the water,
Live the adventure...

I get the feeling that You are nervous,
And believe Me, I am nervous too.
I admit we don't know all there is to know
About each other...
So where do We go from here???

What are We going to do???
Let this moment just fade away???
Or Will We Let Love Find A Way???

HOMAGE TO THE ANCESTORS

How can I speak of Myself
Without first speaking of You

How can I stand proud and strong
In The Presence of men
Without first humbling Myself in Your presence

How can I say this is mine and that is mine
Without first thanking You for giving it to Me

How can I physically touch Myself
Without first spiritually connecting
Myself to You

How can I count the limited years of
My mortal life
Without first counting the limitless years of
Your immortal life

How can I look at the good things
I have and say I enjoy life
Without first looking at the hard times
You had to endure, and still, You enjoyed life

How can I say I have life
Without first understanding that
You made My life possible

How can I be alive
Without first knowing that
You are living in Me

As long as I am alive
You will never die

I AM BLACK

I Am Black,
With My Wide nose and thick lips.
Let's face the fact, I am ugly, I
Hate Myself.
I am ignorant of the true knowledge
Of Myself. I am lazy.
I hate My Black Sisters and Brothers,
I even go around killing them.
I would rather work for a white man
And say no to a Brother.
I would rather buy from a white man
And let My Brother sink in the gutter.

We were miseducated to hate Ourselves.
The fact that Our Ancestors were held
As slaves in america and The Caribbean,
Humiliated, degraded, mistreated, and
Miseducated, trained Us to hate Our
Afrikanness, Our Afrikan race.
But, the plan of the ALL MIGHTY has
Been revealed.
We must start to move.
We must Love Ourselves,
Support Ourselves,
Help Ourselves,
Protect Ourselves,
And Live together in Peace with Ourselves.
Then and only then can We as an Afrikan race
Turn Our fullest attention towards
World Solidarity.

RasTafarI

IF I HAD MY WAY

If I Had My Way, I would just work and play,
And enjoy the day as ordinary people do;
I would make playful use of leisure, pursue
My childhood dreams and pleasures, and
Live for wild and exotic adventures. This is
What I would do, If I Only Had My Way.

If Only I Had My Way, I would only sing songs
That give Me pleasure; I would sing about crazy
Sexy love, holding and rubbing and squeezing tight,
And giving good loving all through the night. This
Is what I would do If Only I Had My Way.

If I Really Had My Way, I would just write poems
About nature; I would write about the
Bright colored rainbow, the flowers
And the bees, and the birds that fly. I would
Write about the Early Morning Sun and The Big
Yellow Moon, and the beauty that they give to
The heavenly sky. This is precisely what I would
Do, If I Really Had My Way.

But I Don't Have My Way, so I must kneel and pray,
Give Thanks and Praise to THE MOST HIGH GOD, who
Has guided and protected Me throughout My Life.
I must make good use of leisure, give to the
Best of My ability, and offer a helping hand to
Women, men, and humanity. These are the
Things that I must do.

I must not only sing songs of Love but also
Redemption Songs, Songs Of Freedom; songs of
Peace, not war, songs of Love not hate, and I must
Also sing Black Songs, songs about My People.
And if I do sing songs about Love, I must sing

About Righteous Love, Eternal Love, and Divine
Love. These are the songs that I must sing.

Writing poems about nature gives Me spiritual
Pleasure; but I must also write poems about
Struggle, The Struggle of My People, past and
Present. I must also write poems about injustice,
And encourage humanity to Sow Some Seeds Of
Justice; and I must write poems about Truth, that
We may learn to seek Truth and Set Ourselves Free.

RasTafarI

LASANA
(Poet Of A People)

I Am LASANA, "Poet Of A People," I write
To My People, about My People, and I humble Myself
And say, I write for My People.

I write what My People feel; My People feel anger,
So I write anger. My People feel Love, so I write
Love. My People feel pain and sorrow, so I write
Pain and sorrow. My People feel joy and happiness,
So I write joy and happiness. My People seek
Truth and Justice; therefore, I write Truth and
Justice. My People are Righteous by nature;
Therefore, I write to Our divine nature.

My People are down; I seek to pick Us up.
My People are dead, I seek to raise Us from the
Grave. My People are lost in the darkness of
Lies, I try to tell Us the Truth, show Us the way,
And give Us a guiding light.

My People are tired and weak, I give Us a place
To rest that We may regain Our strength. My
People pray; I pray with them. My People are
Divided, I want Us to unite.

My People are forgiving, compassionate, caring,...,
I love that about Them. My People are Great, I tell
The world about Them, I am proud of Them, I am
A part of Them, They are a part of Me.

Although I Am LASANA, I am not the originator
Of what I write. JAH IS THE ORIGINATOR, so I too
Must feed from what I write, that I too, might be
Raised from the grave.

LIFE

Life. Life is but a drop of water; it moves
Swiftly, then it is gone. We must live life
To its fullest, but We should live it Uprightly.
No One can live life perfectly; that's why
We must live it in GOD'S LIGHT. We must be
Obedient and Submissive to GOD'S WILL for Us.
We must cherish life and try to keep it for a
Long time. Life. Life is but a drop of water,
It moves swiftly, then it is gone.

NATURE'S BODY

Your eyes are like the moon,
So powerful it draws me closer
To you day by day.
Your hair glitters like a diamond
At the sight of light.
Smooth as the precious Black Coral,
Your body against mine feels so lovely.
And although the moon and the sun
May fade away,
You will be with me every hour
Of every day.

ONE UNIVERSE

We All Are One, One Universe.
Let Us get together under THE MAN.
We must hide our pride and find
Our SMILE.
Let Us play in harmony like the piano's
Keys; We can make good music, let's
Try, and You'll see.
We All Are One, One Universe!!

SUNNY DAY

I love to see a sunny day,
Not filled with rain or snow.
I admire the clear blue sky,
But when it's gray, it makes me cry.
I adore the sun that shines so bright,
And makes the moon light up at night.
And when the sun fails to shine,
I'll close my eyes and say goodnight.

WIND

As strong as I am, It sometimes blows
Me off my feet.
When It reaches its full potential, It
Destroys everything in Its path.
While It's so powerful, it can become
Very gentle, to carry a feather with grace.
We depend on it for energy and comfort.
It's a wonder, something so powerful and
Gentle cannot be seen.

MIRAGE IN THE SKY

Everyone is looking to Heaven for
The answer, but they are looking for
Heaven in the wrong place. They
Are waiting for a man to fall from
The sky; they are watching for a
Mirage In The Sky.

Scores are on a journey trying to
Get to Heaven, but they are traveling
Towards the land of milk and honey.
They are dreaming of building a
kingdom in the sky; they are seeking a
Mirage In The Sky.

Lots of people want to go to Heaven to live
Their life thereafter, but they are all
Quick sprinters running a losing race.
They are all wondering how high they'll
Be able to fly; they are hoping for a
Mirage In The Sky.

Many can't wait to reach Heaven's gate,
But when they get there, they'll be too late;
It was only a Mirage In The Sky.

Countless can't wait to walk those streets of gold,
But when they take a step, they'll fall in a hole;
It was only a Mirage In The Sky.

RasTafarI

MOTHER AND CHILD
(Mama Afrika)

I saw My Mother Afrika crying by the sea,
I went and sat down beside Her, and said:
Hello Mama Afrika. How are You?
I see tears swell in Your eyes. Can You
Tell Me why do You cry?

As She turned and looked at Me, Her face
Began to glow with a smile. As the tears
Ran down the wrinkles on Her face,
I could tell She was crying for me.
As Her tears of sorrow turned to tears
Of Joy and Happiness, She said to Me:

My Child, over 400 years ago, I sat down
Here. I watched as My Children left the
Shores of Their Homeland, the comfort of
My bosom. Some were sold, and some were
Outright stolen; taken away from Me against
Their will. My Children were gone, held captive
In foreign places, were made slaves by
The whiteman.

Taken from Their Wholy land and carried away
Into a strange land; stripped of Their Names
That I adorned, robbed of Their Culture and
Stories of old that I told. Some say it's all apart
Of THE MASTER'S Plan, some put the blame on
The whiteman and some just think it was an
Unfortunate situation.

And now the condition that My Children
Are living under is the worst it has ever
Been since the beginning of Their sojourn
In the west. My sons are labeled as an
36

Endangered species, They are killing One
Another; My Daughters are strung out on crack,
They are being misused and abused by men
And society. My unborn children are crying
Out to Me from the womb of Their Mothers,
They just want a chance to live. But this is
Not why I cry. My cry is a cry of Joy and
Happiness, and not a cry of sorrow.

I cry because many of My Children are coming
Together in Unity. They are putting down Their
Guns and taking a second look at Their condition
Their situation. They are making a bold effort
To bring about a positive change in Their
Community. They are beginning to understand
That the whiteman will never truly help Them.
I see My Children sitting together, pledging to
Unite under a common purpose, despite Their
Different religions, all working towards the
Liberation and Unification of All Afrikan Peoples.

I cry My Child because so many of My Children
Are talking about returning Home. Returning to
Fill the emptiness of My bosom. They yearn for
Me like I long for Them. To sustain My Children
Is My Everlasting purpose, wanting Them to
Return Home is My constant hoping.

RasTafarI

Livicated To The Memory Of Peter Tosh

OBSTACLES OF SLEEP

As I lay My Head down to sleep at night,
Another day says to Me goodnight.
I hear a Mother's cry, Mourning for
Her Son, He just died.
That silent cry I hear so loud,
Comes from afar, traveling in the clouds.
But when I listen carefully to that mourning cry,
I realize it's only the wind howling.

As I turn and lie on My side,
I hear the dripping of Blood. Another
Brother got shot, He stumbles in the Street.
The drips get louder and louder as I try
To fall asleep.
Then I realize the dripping I hear
Is coming from the faucet in My bathroom.

Changing My position and turning on My back,
I hear an infant's faint chuckle that turns
Into a loud cry.
She's alone in a dark alley; Her Mother,
Still, a child runs down the street.
It's Her only choice.
As I toss and turn, I realize
It's the baby next door, crying in the
Middle of the night, Her diaper needs
To be changed.

Obstacles Of Sleep,
Are ringing in My Brain.
Obstacles Of Sleep,
My People won't let Me fall asleep.

SIT IN SILENCE

Learn To Sit In Silence,
And let the sounds
Of nature rejuvenate Your spirit.
Let the singing of Birds, crickets,
And frogs keep Your mind, body,
And soul in Perfect harmony.
Let the roaring Sea remind You of
Your Tenacious Spirit, and the wind,
Your Rhythmic Nature.
Learn To Sit In Silence,
And be at Peace with Your CREATOR.

Learn To Be Silent,
And let Your Words not be heard.
Speaking out Of season may confuse
Your listener and may even confuse You.
The sun Does not shine at night,
Nor does The moon, shine at day;
But when The time is right,
The Will of JAH must be obeyed.
Learn To Sit In Silence,
And be obedient to Your CREATOR.

Learn To Listen and be silent.
Remember that JAH and JAH alone
Is The best knower. Listen and be silent;
For wisdom can be found in the Elders
And in the Youths; and learning can be found
In the Professor and the Homeless
On the Street. Learn To Sit In Silence, and
Seek the Wisdom and Knowledge of Your CREATOR.

RasTafarI

SON RISE

Come On Black Man, take that Mighty Stand;
Don't leave Your Black Woman behind to
Linger, take Her by the hand.

The Original Man, Father of all Mankind.
The First Teacher of the entire world,
The First to explore east, west, north,
And south; the mysteries of the universe You
Know, no doubt! The Generator of GOD
HIMSELF.
You Black Man, It's You I'm speaking about!

The Dominant One, able to produce the Recessive
Ones, but none can produce You. The Master
Architect, The Master Mathematician; The Master
Of Theology, The Master of Astronomy and Astrology.
The Master Teacher of Socrates, Pythagoras,
Aristotle; Yes, The Black Man Herodotus
Spoke of.
You Black Man, It's You I'm speaking about!

The First Kingman to develop civilizations and
Systems of government. The One who prevails with
The Greatest of all Knowledge and Wisdom. Even
Today all doctors of medicine must humbly bow
And honor Imhotep, a Black Man, known to be the
Father of medicine and was also a Master Architect.
You Black Man, It's You I,m speaking about!

Omegas, Alphas, Sigmas, Kappas are all Sons of
Yours Black Man; Deltas, Alphas, Zetas, Sigmas are
All Your Daughters Black Man.
While Crossing the Burning
Sands of the Sudan from Nubia into Egypt, We grew
In knowledge and wisdom.

40

You Black Man, It's You I'm speaking about!

Hey World, wake up! The dawn of the New Day is
Here. The Black Man, along with His Black Woman
Is rising, Powerful and Strong. His Rays will be
Felt throughout the universe, His wrath will come down
On all downpressors. Shine Black Man Shine; The Plan
Of The ALL MIGHTY shall be revealed thru You
And thru Me.
The world is waiting on You, Black Man.

THE GIZAH
(The Great Pyramids)

The Gizah stands Strong
With all of its greatest Mysteries still unsolved.
The sands of time have come and
Gone, still, The Gizah shines on.

Arise as The Gizah rose,
Stand firm like The Gizah Stands,
Be like The Gizah, open yet mysterious.
Silver and Gold, Diamonds and Rubies
Were stolen from The Gizah, still The Gizah
Is Rich, The Gizah is Majestic, The Gizah
Is King, The Gizah is Queen.

May Your Life be as The Gizah in all
Of Your dealings, works, and deeds.
Let Your Home, Your Family, stand strong
As The Gizah.
Let Your Friendships endure and last
As the Gizah.
Let Your mysteries be known to the worthy,
And to the unworthy...be a mystery.

For Wesley and Family

TRAIN

I hear the sound of a train;
I hear its whistle in the wind,
And its rumbling is felt under My Feet.

I don't see the train, but I know it's
Close;
I can't tell if it's coming or going.
Is it bringing Our future or taking
Away Our past?

If it has passed, let Me chase it down,
Because it has something that I need.
If it's on its way, I must make sure
It gets here safely.

People of Afrikan descent, You have to
Know Your past, Know Yourself, and know
Where You came from; for You will not
Know where to go, who You are, and will
Have no future.

RasTafarI

WAR AND PEACE

You say Peace, I say War.
War is the Mother of Peace,
And Peace is the Offspring of War.
When We are seeking Peace,
We must expect to engage in War;
When We engage in War,
We must know that in the end
There will be a time of Peace.

You say Peace, I say Justice.
Justice is the opposite of injustice,
And injustice is the opposite of Justice.
When We are the victims of injustice,
We will wage War;
When We wage War,
We must know that in the end
Justice Will serve all of Humanity.

I say Peace, and You ask, Why?
Peace is the way of JAH.

WHO RULE

Who Rule! RasTafarI Rule
KING Of Kings LORD Of Lords
CONQUERING LION Of The Tribe Of Judah
Elect Of GOD
Earth Rightful Ruler

Yes, King TafarI Rule
HE rides upon the heavens
The KING Of Glory
Strong and Mighty
Mighty In Battle

The KING Of Glory Thundereth
The Voice Of JAH RASTAFARI Is Powerful
And full of Majesty

In His Temple I an I will forIver speak of His Glory
Haile Selassie I sitteth upon His Throne
Yes Selassie I sitteth KING
ForIver

MY SHARI AMOR

"My Shari Amor"
You Are That Bright Spot
That Shines
When Everything Else
Around Me
Goes Gray

The Highlight Of My Week Days
Is To Hear Your Tender Voice
And Southern Twang
Saying "GOOD MORNING DAVIE"
And On The Weekends
I Wonder
What Is Shari Up to

When You Cry
Your Tears Are Like
Rain Drops On My Head
You Have Watered My Life
Made My Spirit Anew

My Heart
Is As Wide
As The Universe
But You Have Filled It
With Your Essence
And Now It Overflows
With Admiration Respect
Friendship And Love
Only For You

CHAPTER II
I AM AFRICAN
- *Poems by Dean L. Weeks* -

ENTER-NET
(Part I)

Tami...

Suddenly in an instant, there you were. As vivid
as any imagination. As real as real can get. As real
as licking the taste of a honey-bun from my fingers.
Mmmm.

You came to me, not in a dream, but by a single thought.
I saw you through the eyes of someone else, but yet it was
you that I saw. I would have paid anything to see your
smile. I almost gave the shirt off my back as an offering.

I cautiously raced to find a point somewhere at the crossroads
where our paths would soon find common ground and there
would be no uncertainty as to why we were there.

My days are filled with enchantment as I hurry home to feel
your thoughts, read your mind, and reflect on what our next
encounter would be like. As I lay my thoughts against yours, I
can't help but to feel your fingers as they caress my soul, as you
touch me in the right place.

With anticipation, I undress the raptor that separates us, as
hours become minutes, minutes turn into seconds and the
miles that lay between us are just a breath away.
Shhhhh. Say no more. The wait is killing me; softly.

With every touch, you cause an erection of my spirit, sending
me soaring through the universe in a climactic state. As I too
begin to touch you and probe every corner, every contour, every
part of you, your heart responds unselfishly to every touch, every
stroke, every part of me.

I imagine the smell of your hair and the tenderness of your skin.

49

My senses tell me that I am in for a treat of one million roses, the smell of sweet lavender. Even the sound of your voice sends silently whispered thoughts through my mind. I can't help but contend with the naked truth that my passion seems energized by the passion within you.

To be Continued......

FROM WHENCE WE CAME

Deep in the *Valley of Dry Bones, where our ancestors lay.
Where the battle of nations was fought. When Kings and
Queens ruled the land. From whence we came.

When our drums were mightier than the distant sound of thunder.
And elders often spoke of the past as if it was yesterday.

We were diverse in our language, colorful in appearance, and
patient with developing civilizations. Where we stood, the
universe was our classroom, the world was a stage, and the
key of life unlocked the gateways of the mind. From whence
we came.

From whence we came. All things in the universe had an
established order. Religion had no recommended boundaries,
limitations, or ending. The mysteries were infinite, all
encompassing. It included specifics about the living and the dead;
laws of life and the afterlife.

Standing on the merit of our good deeds, not on the backs
of our misfortunes. Our veins are rich with the blood of souls,
kindred spirits, and tender hearts.

A certain innocence lurks about us when we consider the
vastness of the River Nile as it stretched forth its arms to
nurture our kingdom. And let us reflect on the uniqueness
and complexity that built the great pyramids. From whence
we came. We were honored as Gods, masterful teachers, and
skillful in our deeds.

We come from a culture-bound and enumerated by the hands
of time. When dynasties ruled the land for centuries. When
science,
astrology, and physics were mere infants in the minds of the
citizens.

Where we once stood as a nation is not lost. We must reclaim our dignity and pride. We must also reassure our existence in this time if we are to journey through the continuum of this life.

HOW COULD WE IGNORE

LIKE THE SMELL OF A THOUSAND ROSES AND THE
STING OF A HUNDRED BEES, SOMEHOW WE HAVE
FOUND A WAY TO IGNORE WHAT WE HAD.

O.K. IT WASN'T SET IN STONE, NOR WAS IT FINAL, BUT
LIKE THE ROAR OF A MIGHTY LIONESS, SOMEHOW I
IGNORED YOUR CALLING.

MAYBE IT'S BECAUSE I HAD FALLEN INTO A DEEP
SLEEP, OR MAYBE IT'S BECAUSE I WASN'T LOOKING IN
THE RIGHT PLACES. HOW COULD WE IGNORE EACH
OTHER?

WE SHARED MORE THAN JUST SPACE AND TIME. AT
ONE POINT WE SHARED EACH OTHER. WE TOUCHED, WE
HUGGED, WE KISSED, AND WE LOVED. ALTHOUGH IT
ONLY HAPPENED ONCE, I HAVE CONTINUED TO LOVE
YOU FROM A DISTANCE.

I AM AFRICAN

I AM NOT MALCOLM X.
I AM NOT MARTIN LUTHER KING.
I AM ME, A SOLDIER.
I AM AFRICAN.
I AM AFRICAN AMERICAN.
I AM AFRICAN CARIBBEAN AMERICAN.
I AM KING DAVID'S GREATER SON, THE POWER OF THE
HOLY TRINITY.
IN ME LIES GENERATIONS OF COLOR, SHADES OF
BLACK.
I HAVE ENDURED THE WHIPS OF INHUMANITY,
CHAINED BY THE LINKS OF PREJUDICE.
I AM A KING. KING OF KINGS. A MIGHTY LION, ROARING
FOR PEACE AND JUSTICE.
I AM ME. UNIQUE AND SPECIAL.
THERE IS NO OTHER.
I STOOD AT THE FOOT HEELS OF HARRIET TUBMAN'S
UNDERGROUND RAILROAD.
I WATCHED, AS IMHOTEP PLANNED AND SHAPED THE
GREAT PYRAMID OF EGYPT.
I WAS A BELIEVER IN THE DREAM, AND I FLEW WITH
THE BUTTERFLY AS HE STUNG AS A BEE.
I, AM ME. A DESCENDANT OF MOTHER AFRICA. SON OF
THE ZULUS, FATHER TO THE RIVER NILE.
I WAS MADE IN THE IMAGE OF H.I.M. THEREFORE I AM
THAT I AM.
A GATHERER OF SEAS AND KEEPER OF SOULS.
I AM AFRICAN.
I AM AFRICAN AMERICAN.

I

I stand before the counsel of the ungodly, bearing witness of His Majesty Emperor Haile Salassie I.

I stand in the presence of the Almighty, King Alpha, and Queen Omega, the beginning and the end. The all knower, the all seer.

I come to overstand that in this time, I will be looked upon, not having to show myself approved unto Jah, but unto the eyes of man. Constantly down, trotting against the rastaman, bingi man, the Lion.

Yea, though I walk through the *Valley of Dry Bones, I know no evilness, for the shadow of my faith surrounds me.

Manifestations of judgment have been established by Jah kingdom. Still, man can not withstand the urge to exalt himself over Jah's rule.

I am that I am. Made in the likeness and image of his likeness, his image: an eternal flame, a consummate burning bush.

Through his mercy and grace, I stand alone. Through his Glory, I shall inherit all of the riches of the earth.

I have stood the test of time. Marcus, a prophet, would know of his coming. Marley would sing of his being. I can serve as a witness to his presence.

I have made and committed myself to a vow, that until the days be separated…,

"I"

MOUNT ZION IS THE FOUNDATION

RasTafarI establish Earth's Rightful Ruler, King Of Kings And Lords Of Lords, God Elect.

King Alpha, Queen Omega, The beginning shall establish the end and the end shall be of the beginning.

The Conquering Lion Of The Tribe Of Judah shall inherit the earth and all the goodness therein. And the rivers of Babylon shall not diminish the path of righteousness.

'Til the days Of Jah Kingdom's Glory and the days of separation, Iman shall vow to continue to seek Jah Light and Guidance.

Look to Mount Zion, for Jah shall come from the hills, armed with deliverance, vengeance, and compassion. I and I will make mention of Rehab and Babylon to the children that know I.

Send forth Jah spirit and Jah herb for the service of his children.

Iman hear from a distance moving in the wind, Nyabingi, Nyabingi. Nyabingi Drums bring word of good news, "Behold Philistia and Tyre, with Ithiopia, This Man was born there."

His foundation is in the Hola Mountains, and Zion and Earth shall be as one. I and I know that Jah RasTafarI shall bring peace unto this earth and move all oppressor Man from the land.

Mount Zion is the Foundation. I lay my dreads upon its bosom and establish Jah kingdom over all nations. SELAH

MY ROAD

I'ma build me a road that's paved with the suffering of my people. Dirty with the blood of my ancestral kingdoms and the dust of the dead.

I'ma build me a road filled with love, understanding, and peace. One that knows no war or turmoil. A road that stretches to the far ends of the earth and the corners of the motherland.

I'ma build me a road that is only black with no white lines to take me places in which I choose not to be or go.

MYSTICAL DREAMER

As I dream of the possibilities, I often dream in color.
I dream of a song, 'cause I've never felt this way about Lovin',
never felt so good, never felt this way about Lovin' it feels so
good."
The possibilities seem endless.

Tailored and spun by the very hands of the Gods, our destiny, our
faith, and our salvation have been blessed by prayer. A prayer sent
from a distant heart, a lonely beat, and a beacon of hope; that an
angel would one day come.
When I dream, I dream in color.

How could such an angel be among men and not benefit from her
glory? Why would anyone not want to soar against her wings?
Why not take a trip towards eternity and forever be happy. You
see, when I dream, I often dream in color.

NOTICE ME

Wandering eyes, eloquent soul seeker, and mate finder. What are
the principles and properties that make up your foreverness?

What do you look for? Who is your Mr. Right, your Dr. Love, your
Brother consciousness? What is the quickest way to your heart?
What is the most direct route to your pleasure center?

Sugarplum Kandi, bubble gumdrop. Skin so soft, it can make a
crocodile jealous, so sweet it reminds me of honey. Honey, for
which coincidentally, I sprinkle all over your body.

The features that I see in you, no other could imagine. No one else
has seen; no one else could ever know. I've noticed you. Why
haven't you caught me?

NIGGERS WANT TO BE NIGGAS

Name-calling,
Jive talking, hip-hop walking
Slip and sliding.
Brothers want to be niggas
Sisters want to niggas
Brothers, sisters
Brothers calling brothers niggas
Sisters calling sisters niggas

Getting mad
Getting mad

Niggers want to be niggas

Niggers want to get mad when a white man calls him a nigger,
somehow suggesting their use of the word is not acceptable, but
niggers want to be niggers,

Niggers want more jobs, but niggers won't stay off the block
Forty-ounce drinking
Long pants wearing
Reefa smokin'

Niggers want to be niggas

BUT OF COURSE
WE HAVEN'T MET YET

All Of A Sudden There You Were.
It's Like You Stepped Out Of A Page
From My Imagination.
But Of Course, We Haven't Met Yet.

All The Things That I Ever Hoped For,
You Seem To Be.
And All The Things I Seem To Be,
You May Be The One That I Hoped For.
But Of Course, We Haven't Met Yet.

Natural To The Bone,
And Sweet As Purple Lavender,
You Are The Cream For My Coffee,
The Sugar For My Tea.
But Of Course, We Haven't Met Yet.

With A Voice As Soft As The Wind
And Powerful Enough To Command
Cleopatra's Army,
You Are The Nile That Flows Within
My Heart From A Distance.
But Of Course, We Haven't Met Yet.

Your Hair Smells Like A Million
Sandalwood Trees,
Your Body Carved By The Hands
Of Perfection.
But Of Course, We Haven't Met Yet.

My Thoughts Become Real
With Anticipation.
And My Hopes Seem Impatient,
I Only Dream Of The Possibilities.

But Of Course, We Haven't Met Yet.

As Time Draws Near
And The Universe Begins To
Surround Me,
Destiny Has Lulled The Fire
Within My Soul.
Spirit Dancer, Oh Queen
Of Mother Earth,
Let Me Wash Away The Pain
From Your Feet.
Let Me Rub Away Your Emotions
And Let Me Touch Your Soul.
But Of Course,...
In Fact, Let's Just Meet.

THE POWER OF THE HOLY TRINITY IS LOVE

THROUGH THE POWER OF HIS IMPERIAL MAJESTY, JAH RASTAFARI KNOW THAT ALL THINGS MUST TAKE HEED TO THE DIVINE POWER OF THE HOLY TRINITY. ALL LIVING CREATURES BIG AND SMALL, MAN, WOMAN, AND CHILD COME TO KNOW THAT LOVE PREVAILS OVER ALL THINGS.

LOVE CAN CONQUER WARS AND RUMORS OF WARS. LOVE MEK' A BLIND MAN SEE, MEK A DEAF GIRL HEAR. LOVE CAN ESTABLISH MANY GENERATIONS TO COME.

LOVE IS A THING THAT CAN CONQUER HATE. LOVE SHALL BE THE HEAD CORNERSTONE FOR THE INHERITANCE OF THE EARTH.

THROUGH THE POWER OF THE HOLY TRINITY, I MAN COME TO KNOW THAT HIS IMPERIAL MAJESTY IS CHRIST RETURNED. I MAN KNOW THAT THROUGH H.I.M I AN I SHALL RULE OVER ALL CREATURES AND ALL THINGS. I AN I KNOW THAT RASTAFARI IS FINAL.

SELAH

CHAPTER III
DON'T PUT ME IN A BOX

BLAME IT ON THE DEVIL

Sometimes I feel sorry for the devil
Cause often he gets blamed
For our lack of responsibility
And for unfavorable situations
We place ourselves in

EXTREMES OF MY HEART

Hard as a rock, soft as water
These are the extremes of my heart
Which one you encounter
Depends on you

SUMMER GLOW

She was sitting on a bench
Outside a lovely wine bar in Italia
On a hot summer day
I stopped and paid her compliments, "You Are Glowing!"

She said, "Thank you, the sun always makes me glow."
I said, "Nah, You make the sun glow!"

I tipped my hat, "Have a wonderful day!"

THE MOON WINKED AT ME LAST NIGHT

Last night the moon winked at me
As I looked up
She crescented her eye
And winked at me
If you only could have seen
The blush she put on my face

BLESSED

She walked up to me and said,
"God Bless You,
For being so independent."

Now, who can take that blessing
Away from me!
Who will fix themselves
To bring a curse against me!
"Who JAH has Blessed,
No man can curse."

I conquered death
From My Mother's Womb,
So don't be fooled by the
Physical me that you see,
I can be dangerous.

I'm not perfect,
I'm not a saint nor a prophet,
Or anything like that;
I'm just a man, just an example
Of what JAH can do
Through you and me.

So I dare to say
JAH sent me from Zion,
I dare to say,
I am Truely Blessed.

RastafarI

BUN DEM BRIDGES
(The Great Dilemma)

The cliche goes, something like...
"Never burn your bridges,
Behind you."
But there are things you should never
Want to return to, after you've
Left them behind

So I say, Bun Dem Bridges
That had a negative hold on you
Bun Dem Bridges
That kept others from seeing
The light of JAH radiating from you

Bun Dem Bridges
To those bad habits, you practice no more
Bun Dem Bridges
To those that spoke evil against you
Burn The Bridges
To cocaine and crack
And all the smack
Cigarettes and alcohol
And weed if you left that
Behind too

Many bridges lead to great places
Just as many can lead to nowhere
At the crossroads is the great dilemma
Right, left, or straight ahead
And the bridge behind
What are we going to do?

FEEL MY NATURE RISE

It's been a long time,
Since I felt my Nature Rise

Oh, how I love that feeling
When My Nature Rise
It starts from deep down inside
And manifests itself
Powerful and Strong

Sometimes it's a touch,
Or something beautiful in my sight
That stimulation I get,
Sends inspiration to my head

Any time of the day
It doesn't matter where I am
Or what I am doing
Taking a shower, driving in my car,
Sitting at my desk at work
Or waking in the middle of the night

When the mood is right
No matter when no matter where
I can't contain myself
I just let it flow
Sometimes like a mighty river
Sometimes like an easy stream
Drip drop, drip drop, drip drop

When My Nature Rise
I like to go deep,
Cause I have no fear;
The deeper the feelings,
The deeper the emotions,
The deeper the message

Yea, it's been a long time,
Since I felt my Nature Rise
It's been a long time,
Since I put Pen to Paper.

IN THE FLOW

I don't need to take a draw
From a good ole ganja spliff
I don't need to take a sip
From my bredren's chalice
I don't need to smoke
A stalk of sensimilla
If I want to express myself
On a Higher Meditation

You see
Not every Rastaman is a ganja man
And not every ganja man is a Rastaman
As it's been said
RastafarI is a Devine Inception
Of Our Hearts

The inspiration of JAH flows thru my head
Sometimes it's heavy, sometimes it's light
This is how I get my high, good vibrations
Picking up heavy inspirations

Right now
I'm In The Flow
Ready to chant down babylon
For the last time
Causing a spark
With the friction I create
As I scratch these words
On paper with my pen
I am ready to set babylon
A blazing fire

babylon "con"tinues to "con" us
War is the means to free" dom"
Keep your free"dom"

And give me Livity
Keep your holy war
And give me revolution
Yes, give me revolution
That I may revolutionize my mind
And be mentally free
Give me revolution
That I may revolutionize my spirit
And be spiritually free

The truth can be an offense
But RastafarI come to put babylon
On weak defense
Sowing seeds of truth
That we may conquer all lies
Sowing seeds of truth
That we may free our minds
Break the chains of mental bondage

Although we know, it's impossible
To go living thru the past
It's time for us to burn all his-torical lies

Sisters and Brothers
They taught Us about christopher columbus
But they did not teach us about the Moors
The Blacks who gave columbus
His knowledge of the sea
They taught us about 1492
But know that this is not the beginning
Of Our-story for you and me

Yes, come let us chant down babylon
For the last and final time
As in the days of Joshua, let us chant
Until the walls of Jericho fall

MR. HAZELNUT

I need to feel something warm and natural.
Yes, I want to feel your strong pleasure.
Deep inside of me tonight.

I want to taste you between my lips,
As you release your smooth liquid flavor,
Slurp Awww!
You are worth every sip.

Mmm, how I love the taste of you
Inside of me, giving me that special sensation
Filling me up just right.

You always have something special for me,
What would I do without you?
You warm me when I am cold,
And you do the job right,
Every morning and night.

Mr. Hazelnut,
You are that something special,
That hot something special
I just love to embrace.

You make me feel so good early in the mornings,
When I wrap my hands around your warm body.
And when you ease inside of me,
All I can say is, YESSSS!

My body is feenin for you right now,
Cause maan you make me glow,
You brighten and warm my day.

I am damn sure ready for you,
Cause I need you more than you want me.

You are good, you taste good, you smell good
And you just downright feel good;
Damn, you are such a sight; I can feel you now.

Ohh how I love to go down and see my man,
Ohh how I love to go down and taste your sweetness,
Ohh how I love to go down and make my Mr. Hazel nut.

* Words by Tina Finley —edited by David L. Weeks

SHINING PRINCE

Our shining Prince has left this world
To take comfort in THE FATHER'S Bosom;
He now sits as a Shining Light
Watching over GoodToBeFriends.

Our family circle may have been broken,
But this is a chance for us to strengthen
Our friendships even more, and renew our
Friendship with GOD.

I have learned in my life that,
"Friendship extends beyond the grave,
And THE FATHER teaches us that,
There is no remembrance in death."

I, like many, was blessed to know Greg,
So GoodToBeFriends, let us remember Greg
In Life, and keep our Friendship with Him alive.

* Livicated To The Living Memory Of Greg Prince

PEN TO PAPER
(Don't Call This A Comeback)

It's been a very long time
Since I put Pen to Paper
More than 3 hundred and 65 days
But don't call this a comeback
This is My Journey forward

Yes, The Inspiration of JAH
Flows from My Head
But I must admit
Inspiration has been scarce
For a long time

A promise made
That became difficult to keep
Led me to this melancholy state
A decision, logical
But still a difficult choice
For my heart to make

It has been a long time
Since the words from my heart and soul
Flowed through the ink of my pen
But I am holding on to my pen
I'm holding to my faith

Slowly but surely
I'm beginning to feel
A tingling in My fingers
A bubbling in My heart
And a stirring in My soul
Like storm clouds
Inspirations are gathering in My head

You can call it writer's block

Or you might say, "his time is up
He's said all he had to say"
But don't you dare call this a comeback
I've been doing this for over twenty years
I'M A VETERAN AT THIS!!

THE PARTY'S OVER

The party's over,
But can we have this last dance?

There won't be any invitations
Back to my place, no exchange of digits
For planning a first date.

If I ever see you again, it would be a coincidence
No, hi, how you doing, only a passing glance.

It was a beautiful experience, while it lasted,
Basking in your heavenly grace.
I know that you were diggin' me,
Cause I felt your spirit touch mine.

You see, I was diggin' you too
No lie, this is truth.
From the minute I saw you
I knew you were a special light
I wanted to spend this whole night
With you

So when that hour strikes
And the DJ plays the last song
I want your body pressing against mine
For tomorrow, this night will be gone

There won't be any invitations
Back to my place, no exchange of digits
For planning a first date.

But!
...Different night, different place
Different time...Until then,... MY SECRET LOVE!

THE TRUMPET

I stood on the mountain top
And have seen the big hand move
From the time of creation
To the time of now
Even to the time to come

Roaming in the valley of darkness
What guides me comes from within
The light of faith, truth, and right
Only those that see by the light within
Will become like the one
That dwells within

Strolling on the banks of the river
The ignorant, unfaithful, and unrighteous
Are dying of thirst
While Marley's trumpet blows, they dance
To the rhythm of the downpressor

I have seen the big hand move
For THE CREATOR Creates
And THE SUSTAINER Sustains
He gave me eyes that I may see
And ears that I may hear.
Look, and you will see the light within
Listen, and you will hear the truth

WOW!

She is a familiar face
From many years gone by
But, WOW!
Some women just get more beautiful
With age and time

PERSPECTIVE

No matter the angle of your close-up profile
Or your smooth curves, in full view
Or the hazy contours of your distant silhouette
From any perspective, any spherical point of view
You are beautiful inside and out!

Top to bottom, front to back, and sideways too
All viewpoints must confess, the truth
You are always In Vogue!

CHAPTER IV
GIVE THE PEOPLE WHAT THEY WANT
- From Me To You -

A CHAIN ONCE BROKEN

Today we all would hope
We didn't have to bear this pain of loss;
And it may be hard for us to see the light,
In this seemingly time of darkness.
But a chain that was once broken
Is now linked again in Heaven

Father and Daughter have joined again,
To share the gift of eternity.
Let us all celebrate and be glad,
A daughter is back in the bosom of her Father;
A man is once again blessed with the duty
Of being there to protect his daughter.

A Will once chained
Is now emancipated from the chains of a disability
A bound spirit is now free from the limitations
Of the body

Yes, we have physically lost,
A family member, a loved one, and a friend;
But Friendship, Love and Family,
These bonds extend way beyond the grave.

Father and daughter,
A Chain Once Broken,
Are joined together again, in Heaven.

IF YOU CRY

If You Cried Yesterday
I hope they were Tears of Joy
Over special times shared
For those are the thoughts
And memories to always cherish

Memories good and bad
Happy and sad, Will always be with us
But If Today You Cry, make Your choice
And let it be memories of happy
And good times had

The psalmist David teaches that,
"There is no remembrance in death"
So, If Tomorrow You Cry
Hold on to the living memories
Hold on to the memories that make you smile

JOY

I remember you; how could I forget those eyes
The first time I saw them, I felt an old familiar Joy
From a time long gone by

A time when, after a long night of anticipation
The Joy felt as it's time to awake and open presents
Christmas just doesn't seem like what it used to be

Seeing those eyes again
I experience that sweet Joy
That comes with the morning light
As I give thanks to GOD
For guiding me through the night

Like having a night of dreams
Of loving thoughts and peacefulness
Then, rising with a Joyful Spirit

How could I forget such a beautiful sun-bright smile
That causes the roses to bloom, flawlessly
The birds to all sing in perfect harmony
And the breeze to blow, soft and steady
Oh yea, it's definitely going to be a Joyful day

How could I forget You
That day, You brought Me JOY!

LIFE IS MADE FOR LIVING

It comes with ups and downs
Happiness and sorrow
Pain and good feelings
But I do believe Life Is Made for Living!

Yes, hold on to loving and joyful memories
But put one foot in front of the other
And keep stepping forward
For there is lots more for you to give
And even more for you to receive.

At quiet times when you sit
Dance to the rhythm of your heartbeat
Smile, just for the hell of it
Laugh out loud, for no darn good reason
Giggle, just because you feel like it
Get up and jump around, even if people
Are staring

Oh, yea! Life Is Made for Living!

VICIOUS TO VICTORIOUS

Jesus to The Christ
This was THE FATHER'S plan
To transform HIS Son
Into a Higher Man
Viscous To Victorious

I have learned
You cannot place new wine
Into old wineskin, so I had to put on
A new Skin, an Upright skin
A skin that will hold The Mighty
Spirit of GOD within

The Slaughtered Lamb died
For my sins, for the sins of the world
Giving His Life as a Salvation
But today, He lives for me
He Reigns with All Power and Authority
The Conquering Lion of The Tribe of Judah
Viscous To Victorious

Viscous To Victorious
This is my transformation
GOD's Destined Plan
For me to live in HIS Will
To speak of HIS Glory
And to testify of HIS Mercy

This is my time to put off the old woman
And to walk in the ways of the new woman
Do not remember the former things
Neither consider the things of old
Behold, Angela is doing a new THING!
Viscous To Victorious

VICTORIOUS WOMAN IN A SEXY RED DRESS

This poem is about a Victorious Woman
In a Sexy Red Dress
You see, she walks in a new light
And for that, I am genuinely impressed

But I like to see Her in That Red Dress
Contrasting nicely with Her caramel brown skin
Flowing smoothly along the lines of Her body's shape

Yes, she changed the ways of her past living
And now embraces Her Divine nature

And seeing Her in That Red Dress
I must confess, makes my heart skip a beat
Makes my emotion run wild and free
And puts an amorous feeling in my soul

By GOD's Grace and HIS Mercy
She made it through the vicious ordeal of a victimizing crime
And now she faces her future Victoriously

Like Matriarchs of Days of Old
Adorned in the royalty of Purple and Gold
She is A Queen
A Victorious Woman
In a Sexy Red Dress!

CHAPTER V
BRING ME A HIGHER LOVE

A PLACE TO LAY MY BURDEN DOWN

Even with a vast heart
That extends far beyond the universe
My Love began to overflow
Having no place to go

A burning desire to share Love
This is the burden that I carry
So I had to find a place
To let My Heart and Love flow

I reached out here, and there
And once again, I had to settle for
"We're just friends"
"You're like a brother to me"
Another broken date
Another request, for a rain check

Time and time again
I ask Myself
Will I ever find a place
To share My Love
A place to let My Love flow
Will I ever find a permanent place
To Lay My Burden down?

BACK TO THE STILL WATERS

Can I take You back
Back To The Still Waters
So We can remember our Roots
Our-story
For like the still waters
Our Roots runs deep

Can I take You back
Back to the beginning
When it was just You and Me
Before the darkness brought forth the light
Long before the serpent in the tree

Before, it took two
Two to make love
Back when We were ONE
When We were LOVE

Do You remember
The time before the river Gihon
Before the river Euphrates
Began to flow
When I was the only river
That flowed into Your sea
Before Sirus, before Orion
When You were the only star
That existed in My night

When You formed Me
In the darkness of Your womb
When I fashioned You
In the palm of My hands

Do you remember
When Making Love was without form
92

Like an eternity, a lasting experience
Without end

I remember you
Do you remember me
Do you remember
When We were WoMan
Do You remember
When We were ONE
Can I take you back
To The Still Waters
Can We Make Love
Like We Used To?
When it was beautiful!

HEAVEN

I knew she was an angel, so I asked,
"When did you leave heaven?"
She said, "I never left!"
My epiphany —I was in Heaven!

Whoever said,
One had to die to go to Heaven,
Is a liar.
How can one enjoy Heaven and be in a grave?
Heaven is Life, Heaven is Beauty, Heaven is Love.

The Psalmist teaches, "Delight yourself in The LORD
And HE will give you your hearts' desires."
So, I will delight myself in JAH Glory,
And HE will give me Heaven, HE will give me You!

LET'S MAKE LOVE
ON VALENTINE'S NIGHT

Let's Make Love
On This Valentine's Night
Surrounded By The Soft Fire Of Candle Lights
Like Wax Before A Fire
We Can Melt Into Each Other, Flowing
Under The Heat Of Our Desire

Let's Keep It A Secret
What We Whisper
As We Make Love To Each Other
In The Passion Of The Night
When Our Bodies Fade
Intimately Into Each Other
And Our Spirits Become One

The Moment When The Rhythm
Of Our Hearts Begin To Beat In Sync
As Our Bodies Meet With Every Stroke
Every Movement Having A Divine Purpose
A Journey To Higher Ecstasy

Let's Make Sweet Love
Under The Haze Of Candle Light
On This Valentine's Night
For Tonight Is Not Just Another Ordinary Night
Tonight Is Special, Just For Lovers
To Satisfy Intimate Desires
And Give Loving Pleasure
One To The Other

Happy Valentine!!

LIGHT YOUR FIRE

I was born with the knowledge
Of how to have sex
You know, the vagina and the penis
And how one was designed
To be inserted into the other
It's a natural thing embedded
In every man and woman.

But that is such a primal level
As men and women
We must be on a Higher Level
Surrender to the power of The Spirit
And conquer the cravens of the flesh.

I know about the in and out
The round and round and all about
But what I really wanna know is
How Do I Light Your Fire
How do I take you spiritually higher?

You see, it's easy for me
To get my man
Then roll over and fall asleep
But it's all about You Baby
It's all about what drives you crazy!

Some Sisters like their strokes long
Some like 'em short, some like it fast
Some like it nice and slow
Some like it from the back, and
Some just like it when you L.I.G.

Maybe it might just be a bubble bath
Or back rub, a full body massage
Or some poetry straight from my heart
96

Or just a simple kiss on the lips
It just doesn't matter; I just wanna know what you're
All about, 'cause pleasing you is what pleases me
And that's what I'm all about
Tell me, how do you like your Loving?

How Do I Light Your Fire Baby
How do I take you spiritually higher?
You see, to me, it's more than just a primal act
More than just who can handle who
More than just a competition in bed
It's a heavenly journey
Sacred, just between you and me
Teach me, Baby
Teach Me How To Light Your Fire!

MOTHER NATURE STILL HAS A FEW TRICKS UP HER SLEEVES

New Love
It is like a sunrise, more beautiful
Than ever before
As it rises over the mountain top
Like a multi-colored rose that suddenly appears
Challenging the norm, exciting the possibilities

If you've seen one rose,
You've seen them all.
But now and then,
One comes along
That's unique and unexpected

Mother Nature Still Has A Few Tricks Up Her Sleeves
So, I will stand firm and be steadfast
And believe that there is someone special
Made just for me

An extra spectacular sunset
A moon with a more mellow glow
A rose that's like no other
Extraordinary!

Someone full of patience
Loving and kind at heart
My companion, My lover
My friend

You see,
There's always a new star being born
A new galaxy being discovered
Things we don't usually see
Cause Mother Nature
She works in secrecy

So, I will stand firm and be steadfast
And believe that there is someone special
A rose that's like no other, extraordinary
Made just for me

MY FIRST NIGHT WITH YOU

One week ago
We were in each other's arms
Making Love
Oh, what a night it was
Like you said, "A Perfect Starting Place."

The season was right for reaping
For it was months ago
That we planted the seeds of Love,
Never knowing what fruits we would bring forth.

What a special night
For us to share intimacy
To expose ourselves
To Love's possibilities
To reach out and touch
Each others' soul, each others' spirit.

One week ago,
We ventured, and we gained
That night, I found My Angel in You
That night, You were finally comforted to know
That, someone, did find
Your message in that bottle
And you were lying in His arms.

I Will Always Remember, My First Night With You

CHAPTER VI
WORD SOUND, POWER!

CELEBRATING JAH

I accept that the words are mine
But To JAH Be The Glory
For HE Is My Inspiration

I will celebrate JAH
And unto HIM I will pour My spirit
As My libation

My feet will dance with joy
And My voice will sing HIS praises
For HE judges with righteousness
And is Full of forgiveness

I can't say that I have lived a hard life
But I have had, and still have
My share of trials to overcome
Some saw that strength that was in me
But I also had to prove myself to others
Some foolishly mistook me
For just another disabled child
But there has always been those who knew
I was GOD'S Child

For those who tried to confine me
To special education
And for those who never believed
That I would cross those "burning sands"
Shame on you

I will always be Celebrating JAH
For HE has always been with me
From the silence of My Mother's Womb
To this present moment in my life's Journey
I KNOW that JAH will never let me down
And I thank H.I.M. for the positive days

That HE has placed before me

There are many more days ahead of me
Some will be difficult, and some will be trial free
But no matter what
I'll be forever Celebrating JAH
For HE is My Help

COUNSEL ME

All have sinned
And have come short of Your Glory
But, for goodness sake, I will always seek
Your Counsel

I come to You with my sacrifice
A contrite heart and a broken spirit

Deliver me, Oh JAH
From my unrighteous and sinful ways
Guide my steps in the ways of right
That I may walk upright in Your Sight

Grant me the compassion and the love
That I may forgive all those that have
Sinned against me

Help me to walk not
In the way of temptation
Help me to turn aside
From all things that lead me astray

Never let Your presence leave me
I always want to keep You near
So, Lead me with a firm hand
And spare not Thy Rod from me
Less I go astray and fall out of Your Favor

Search my heart....
Examine my soul....
Set me right, if I'm in suspicion

Inspire confidence where there is doubt
Inspire strength where there is weakness
Inspire resoluteness where there is wavering

Inspire action where there is procrastination

"Humble, but not weak
Strong, but not boastful"
Steadfast, yet not intimidating
Patient, yet not inert
These are good qualities
Make them a part of my character
Write them in my heart
O FATHER
Counsel Me In Thy Ways...
SELAH!!!

DRIFTING

In 1987, I sighted JAH
Ever since then, I've been drifting
Drifting towards The Light of RastafarI

In 1988, I vowed the vow of the Nazarite
I threw my comb and brush away
And let the locks of my hair grow
To separate myself unto THE LORD
An upright way of living
Became my constant striving

I made lots of decisions
Some good and some bad
I've been in situations
I damn well knew I shouldn't
Have placed myself in
And I have experienced
Many Positive things
That has changed my life
But through it all
I still find myself drifting
Drifting towards The Light of RastafarI

Good habits, bad habits
I have my share of them
The bad ones, I am determined
To get rid of
The good ones, I will continue
To practice
Nonetheless, in GOD'S Loving Grace
I will continue to stand

Rastalivity is a living way of life
Continually growing, always revealing
And bringing to light the mysteries

Of GOD and life.

That's why I'll always be drifting
Drifting, drifting, drifting
Drifting towards The Light of JAH RastafarI!

HOW MANY MOSES

How many Moses' must it take,
To lead Us across the red sea.
How many rivers do we have to cross,
Before we finally cross over.

Is there no escaping
Pharaoh's mighty army,
Will we forever sit
By these rivers of babylon,
Just weeping over our conditions.

The writing has been on the wall,
Jesus, Marcus, Malcolm, Martin, Peter, and Bob,
When will we heed these messengers' call?

Why should JAH send Us another Prophet,
When in the end, He falls victim
To an assassin's bullet.
Why should JAH sacrifice another Son,
When so many of Us refuse to bear
Our own Cross.

Where there is no vision, the people perish,
So only with a Unified Vision can We prosper.
Why are We still being destroyed for lack of knowledge,
When the truth of Our Afrikan Glory
Shines for all to see.

We don't need another Moses,
The writing's already on the wall.
It's time to write these messages on our hearts,
Free our individual selves
From mental and spiritual bondage.
We don't need another Moses,
Each of Us just needs to be a Moses.

IN MY FATHERS' WILL

I am in The Will of My FATHER,
So it matters not the obstacles before me,
I must prosper.

Clear is the path,
When I look with eyes of faith.
Smooth is the way,
When I make my steps confident.

Bring me my cross, for it is mine to bear,
Though it may be heavy, I will persevere and endure,
For many bore heavier crosses before me.

I am in My FATHERS' Will,
This is the knowledge I should be walking in;
"For in the presence of mine enemies,
HE has prepared my table before me,
And HE will cause my cup to run over."

Long may be the Journey that I face,
Still, I must keep the vision of my Journey's end,
Clear in mind, and make my means to that end
A steady and enduring pace.

Thoughts of failure and fear
Might sometimes distract,
But why worry about them
When I know, I can pray them off.
I am in The Will of My FATHER,
It matters not the obstacles that are before me,
Iman must prosper.

IN MY POETRY

In My Poetry
JAH is the Inspiration
That flows from my head
HE is the clear Message
And the ones written
In between the lines

HE is The Guiding Light
In the dark tunnels of life
HE is the Sweet Comfort
To a battered and broken heart
The Spoken Word
That simply makes Us Smile

In My Poetry
JAH is The Love
That is meant to be shared
Between a man and a woman
And when making love
HE is the heavenly pleasure
HE takes Us spiritually higher

MY CHAPEL

HAILE SELASSIE is My Chapel
In HIM, I let my troubles rest
On my Knees, I pray, and give HIM
Praise and Thanks
For HIS Loving Grace and gift
Of Salvation

When faced with a fork
In the road of life
And temptation clouds my discretion
I turn to HIS knowledge, HIS Wisdom
And HIS Understanding
For guidance in making the right
Decision

With flesh and blood, I do not fight
But over my spiritual enemies
JAH gives me the victory

HE keeps me straight on the path
With a Firm Hand, But whenever
 I stumble and fall, with Gentle Hands
And a Warm Bosom HE cradles me

I always try to walk in HIS Word
Cause I Know They will never lead me astray
In HIM alone do I put All my trust
This way, I know everything will be all right

On My Chapel
I will always lean
My knees will always bend
And my tongue will always confess
That JAH RastafarI Is Alive
Cause I Feel HIS Spirit Inside Of Me! SELAH!

SERVE JAH

Serve JAH in everything that you do,
This way, your works will always be
Upright and True

Man was made to serve THE ALMIGHTY.
Whether you worship HIM as a Christian, Muslim, or Jew
That, my brothers and sisters, is left up to you

Everyone has a right to worship THE FATHER
As they see fit within their own life,
And within their own relationship with HIM.
As a people, we are not monolithic;
So, as uniquely as GOD created each and every one of us,
Just as uniquely our worship of and relationship with HIM,
Should naturally be.

Man, know your roots, know your culture;
Serve JAH within your cultural expression.
My roots and culture
Is of a Black Ancient Tradition,
And I serve JAH within This Foundation!

I do believe, The Desire of THE FATHER
Is to dwell in the hearts of HIS Children, and We in HIM
So strive to keep your temple clean
Some may not believe this, and that's their right to decide
But for Me and My House, We will serve the JAH.

SOMETIMES I ROAR

It's always been a part of my life
There's always someone who foolishly thinks
They can take advantage of me
From the bully on the playground
To the people I meet today
In my adult life

I was born with Cerebral Palsy
So I walk a little un-orthodox
And I have a blurred speech.
Many times, many have seen this
As a "get over" opportunity
Only to realize they've encountered
A strong mind and body

I walk in peace
Agitation disturbs my fragile nerves
From time to time
Some mistake this as timidity
And come at me disrespectfully.
Check yourself!

Yes, love, life and laughter, that's Me
And it's the side of me I prefer all to see
But, Sometimes I Roar
And I just have to release
The Fire side of me

Kind at heart
This is the dominant spirit GOD gave to me
If I become cold as ice
It's because you abused my kind-heartedness
And only time will get you back
Within my good graces

I don't walk this earth with a screwface
Ninety-nine, point nine percent of the time
I got that, Irie Feeling
Yea, that's just the way I move

I am a gentleman
A good human being
Polite, respectful, peaceful
But sometimes, This Lion Has To Roar !!

TRIUMPHANTLY

I no longer hear
The crack of a whip
But still, my blood runs cold
When I remember those
Bottomless slave ships
And how they brutalized
Our souls

Those days
We should never forget!
But, in these times
JAH gives us the power
And the authority
To Move **Triumphantly**
To shape and control our own
Destiny

What is for I
JAH has already written it
In HIS Will for I
And what is for ceasar
babylon will give to ceasar

The Kingdom of JAH is within us all
Yes, The Kingdom of JAH is within I an I
This is what The Master taught
It is up to everyone to establish
This reality, not somewhere in space
But on Earth, right here in Our Community

Why do we still portray Jesus The Christ
As a slaughtered Lamb
Adorning our Churches, our Homes
Our bodies, with crucifixes and crosses

In These Times, Know That
Jesus Reigns **Triumphant**
As The Conquering Lion Of The Tribe Of Judah
Haile Salassie I, Christ In His Kingly Character
KING Of Kings, LORD Of Lords

So, Wear Your Lion
And Represent The Living KING!

There is no more time
For us to sit on the corner and jester
Bickering over the things
babylon will never deliver

Kujichagulia, self-determination
Should be our motivational force
And our guiding star, towards prosperity
That We May Stand With Power And Authority
Triumphantly!

* To The Living Memory Of Robert Nesta Marley

WE SHOULD STILL PRAY

Whether Our skies
Are bright sunny blue
Or thunderstorm gray
We should still give thanks
And pray
Cause somewhere
Along the way
There was a blessing
That brought Us to this day

Yesterday,
Might not have been
A perfect day.
Tomorrow,
We have no real idea
Of what to expect.
But today,
Let Us count
Our many blessings;
For this morning we saw the sun,
Obediently rising once again.
And we felt the chill
In the dew filled air

This morning started dense with fog
But still, I knew I had to tackle the day
So I asked JAH to brighten my vision
Help me see clear through this early
Morning fog
Help me see clear through
The everyday fog
The everyday fog of life
The good & the bad
The obstacles that try to hinder me
The people that try to help me

118

The ones that fight against me
The ones that Truely love me
And JAH, help me to shed my own fog
That everyone can clearly
See me
And Know me
Truely know the man inside me...

WHO IS PRAISING THE LORD?

The Christians, Jews, and Muslims are warring;
Who is praising THE LORD?

I n I Dawtas and Sons
Children of HIS IMPERIAL MAJESTY
Give Thanks and Praise to THE MOST HIGH
And war, we leave that to the mongers

The people put their trust
In presidents, prime ministers, politicians, preachers
And those with a terrorist agenda
RastafarI trust in THE LORD
And delight in All HIS Glory

Yes, Christians, Jews, and Muslims
Are waging war against one another
Each claiming to be backed
By God the Father
Calling on the Father to give them the strength
To conquer the flesh of another human being

Who is seeking THE FATHER
For the sake of uprightness
Who is calling On The Might of JAH
To fight against spiritual wickedness
And to bring the victory of good over evil

Who is seeking GOD'S Mercy, HIS Counsel
Who is praying, "O JAH, search my heart, examine my soul

Who is praising THE LORD?

YOU CANNOT WEAR MY CROWN

There is nothing new under JAH Sun,
But everyone has a unique testimony.

I was born, my skin blue, "suffered at birth,"
There was no oxygen in the first tank,
The second tank, questionable;
This was my Mother's account—
But, I conquered death from Her Womb.
You Cannot Wear My Crown!

Ask me truth, and I'll tell no lie,
"I'd rather not to have been born with
Cerebral Palsy; Still, I have no regrets
Of the life I have lived.

Pick up your own cross,
Mine you are not able to carry;
Don't judge me; you are just not worthy.
"The journey of a thousand miles
Begins with one step", you walk yours
And I will walk mine.

Habits: good and bad, we all have them;
Only GOD knows all the right and the
Wrongs we have done and those things
Will always live with us, no matter what.

As the youngsters say these days,
"Do you" and I'll do me; 'cause in the end,
I cannot stand in judgment for the things you have done
Nor can you stand in judgment for the things I have done.
So strive to live Upful and Right in JAH Sight.

You Cannot Wear My Crown;
And in truth, I cannot wear yours!

CHAPTER VII
I-ROSE
- My Fire Angel -

ANOTHER ANGEL TO WATCH OVER ME

Zion, O Zion
Swing Wide
Open Thy Heavenly Gates
Another Angel Forward to Zion

Now, don't get this confused
With any conceived mythical figures
Draped in white garments
And white feathered wings
That might be in your mind

This Angel is my Mother, The Matriarch
And while She was on this earth
She was A Fiya Woman
She was more like a Lioness
But She was My Lion too
Now She is My Fiya Angel

She loved, protected, and cared for me
And when needed, She fought for me too
When I couldn't stand up for myself
She stood firm for me
My Mother is very much responsible
For where I am today

Zion, O Zion
Swing Wide
Open Thy Heavenly Gates
For JAH has sent Another Angel
To Watch Over Me

No imaginary creatures in the clouds
Playing on golden harps
And singing on heavenly highs

You see, My Angel is an extension
Of Her earthly character
Headstrong and full of Fiya
Yes, My Angel is a Fiya Angel

In Truth, I wouldn't want anyone else
To watch over me
But My Mammie and My Daddie

So tell me, what kind of Angel would you want, watching over
you?
Some white-feathered winged mythical creature
Or Someone That Is REAL To You!

IT'S ALL ABOUT THE DASH

I went to the social security office to take care of my mother's final business. I was the representative payee for my mother. I was responsible for paying all her bills, nursing home, medical, etc. — you know, stuff like that.

When I applied to be the representative payee for my mother, I had to fill out lots of paperwork. I had to get proof of this, evidence of that; I had to get this signed and that signed. So, naturally, when I went back, I expected I would have to fill out more paperwork. The conversation went something like this:

Good morning; I am the payee representative for my mother. She passed away last week, and I am here to take care of any final business.

The receptionist responded, "I am very sorry for your loss. Can I have your Mother's social security number…can I have your social security number. Do you have her death certificate?"

I gave her the information. Then she asked, "Did you receive her deposit for this month?"

I said, "Yes." Then the receptionist said, "Your mother won't receive any more deposits."

I said Ok.

So, I stood there for about a second or two. Expecting she would give me more paperwork to fill out. Then she said, That's it, you're done." I stood looking at her with an expression on my face, "Just Like That?" That is what flashed through my mind. "Just like that. Is that all there is to my mother? A few verbal exchanges, and the exchange of a few sheets of paper?"

I should mention here that this is not about the receptionist; she was very courteous and kind-spoken as can be. It just struck me that the whole process was so dry and uneventful.

As I drove back to work, I had such a sad and uneasy feeling, and my mind began to wander, searching for some kind of comfort. Then something that I have read and heard so many times gave me comfort. I remembered what my Mother's life was really about. It was All About My Mother's "Dash."

MAMMIE'S HOUSE

Oh, how I miss Mammie's House,
For it is the only House I know.
I can remember, in Mammie's House
Not so long ago, when I was,
But didn't know.

I left Mammie's House. The taste of milk,
Mammie's Milk from Mammie's Breast.
Suddenly! What is this? Not Mammie's Milk.
Not even Mammie's Breast; I guess Mammie
Knows best.

I left Mammie's House to go outside
To play. Growing, as I met my
First friends. We played together
Making our friendships stronger. I stumbled
And fell and hurt my knees. To Mammie's
House I ran, for it is the only House I know.
And Mammie made my knees better.

Years later, it was time for me to leave
Mammie's House again. It was time for me
To be One with my destiny. I made mistakes,
I am only human. Striving to be what
I was created to be. Again I stumbled and fell,
But this time, I had to make it better.

Mammie's House is still The Only House I Know.
But now, Mammie's House is no longer there.
Now Mammie's Fire forever burns in My Heart.

I Love You, Mammie!

CHAPTER VIII
WHAT'S LOVE GOT TO DO WITH IT?

JAZZ

I Play Her At Night,
When I Want To Get In The Mood,
You Know, Like When I Want To Let The World Go,
And Let Tranquility In.

The Sweet Sound Of Her Sexy Voice,
The Music That She Plays,
Sets My Emotions Just Right.
And As I Sit Back, Relaxed In My Easy Chair,
She Plays Her Rhythm On My Body
And Takes Me To Her Sensual Place.

Smooth With Her Touch,
Her Fingers Play Mellow Chords
Down My Spine.
She Wraps Her Lips Around Me,
And Blows Me, Playing Me
To A Smooth Saxophone Groove.

Like A Guitarist, She Strums My Strings,
The Most Sensitive Parts Of Me.
I Close My Eyes And Let Myself Fall
Into Her Flow,
As She Takes Me Deeper And Deeper,
Deeper Into Her Quiet Bliss.

Yeah, Jazz.
She Spreads Her Essence All Over Me,
Slides Herself Inside Me, She Unwinds Me.
And With A Melody
That Brings On The Midnight Mood,
She Seduces Me,
And I Slowly Drift Under Her
Black Magic Spells

A LOVE POEM

It's a love poem with a familiar feel
Verse with a universal appeal
Sharing emotions so commonly real
Sounds like love; I know the deal

Maybe because for me
Speaking these words don't come
So easily, I take these words from
My heart, and let them flow
From pen to paper

Forever past Eternal
Steam of passion infernal
Heat enough to burn all
Fear, doubt, and inhibition

From just beyond the light
Appearing before my sight
A man strode into this night
On a quest... A life-long mission.

What has he been missing?

Love,
Simple, Pure, True, Unconditional,
Love...

ACROSS THE MIDNIGHT SKY

Do you ever
Let your mind drift
Across the midnight sky
And think about me
Like I think about you

Are there times
When you say to yourself
I wonder what he is doing
I wonder what he's dreaming

When the sky's hue
Turns to that dark midnight blue
Am I ever a pleasant thought
That recalls a delightful memory
Am I ever a marvelous feeling
That draws a smile

And when the night finally reaches
To morning blue
Did you dream of me
Like I dreamt of you?

AT THIS ALTAR

At This Altar, We Stand
I Take Your Hands In My Hands
I Put My Hands In Yours
And Proclaim You And Me, One

As We Make Holy This Divine Union
With GOD As Our Counsel And Friends As Our Witness
Let Us Take These Vows In The Presence Of All

Together
We Light This Unity Candle
And Trust In GOD That
From This Day On
Only One Flame Will Burn
Only One Heart Will Beat

This Marriage
Is Not About Promises
Not About Professing, Our Endless Love For Each Other
But Acknowledging The Simple Fact
We Should Be Together
And Not Just Believing
But Knowing
Who GOD Puts Together
No One Puts Asunder

Until Forever Past Eternity
This Love Of Ours Will Last
As We Keep The Love That We Have For Each Other
Rooted, Deep In Our Love For JEHOVAH

* To The Unity Of Veronica And Obi

136

BABY BLUES

You sure are looking good
In those Baby Blues
Hugging every curve of your body
Just right
Top to bottom, back to front
Right now, you are pleasing to my sight.

I pride myself on being a gentleman
And always treating my sisters right
But right now, babe, you are turning me on
I'm trying my best to be humble
But how can I be that
When I'm looking at someone as fine as you

Golden brown skin, legs showing
I'm diggin' the way your body flows
You might as well just call me uncle sam, babe
Cause "I Want You," in or out
Of those Baby Blues.

BUENAS NOCHES

Duerme bien mi amor;
Deja que el espíritu de JAH
Guiarte a través de la noche.

Duerme con los sonidos silenciosos
Que se escuchan solo de noche;
Deja que la brisa de medianoche
Lleva tu alma a
Luz de la mañana.

Que tus sueños
Sean sueños de pensamientos rectos
Y Paz;
Puedes levantarte con
Un espíritu gozoso.

.... No olvides sonreír
En el sol naciente,
Para mostrar su agradecimiento.

CHOCOLATE GIRL

I got myself a Chocolate Girl
And she's the sweetest thing
In my chocolate world
Whenever I'm yearning
For something sweet
I think of my girl and her
Chocolate treats

Like chocolate syrup
Over chocolate ice cream
My chocolate girl pours herself
All over me
Like chocolate milk and
Chocolate flavor "Nestle Quik"
Me and my girl blend
As One

Whenever we get together
My Chocolate Girl and I
Double the chocolate taste
Chocolate on top of chocolate
Chocolate drippin'
From chocolate spaces
Chocolate bars in between
Chocolate kisses
We make a perfect cherry-topped
Chocolate cool whip
Banana split

Yep!
I got myself a Chocolate Girl
And she's the sweetest thing
In my chocolate world
Whenever I'm yearning
For something sweet

I take a taste of My Chocolate Girl
And her chocolate treats

EBONY LATINA

A Beautiful Black Woman
With A Smooth Latin Flavor
Hot Spicy Salsa
With An Afrikan Twist

Her Spirit Shows
Through Her Smile
Compassion Love
And Sensitivity
These Are The Tenets
Of Her Heart

I Imagine Myself
Dancing To The Rhythm
Of Her Walk
When Her Hips Roll
I Hear Afrikan Drums
I Hear A Seductive Beat

She Is A Woman
For All Seasons
Warms Me
On Cold Winter
Nights
Cools Me
In The Hot
Summer's Heat

She Is Like
A Cool Breeze
On A Clear
Spring Day
Like A Chile
In The Air
On A Crisp

Autumn Night

Her Touch
Like Sparks…
….Ignites The Fire
Of Love

QUIET STORM
(Love Scenes)

Evening Sun sets
Giving way to the night
The Moon rises
Mellow with a yellow glow
As if moving to a jazzy groove
Setting the mood for our evening
Of serenity and peace
A night of Quiet bliss

Midnight Blue sky
Deep blue with passion and emotions
In The Mood For Love
Our anticipation
An Intimate Rumble

Warm front, Cool front merge
High pressure, Low pressure settles
Warm air, Cool air entwine
A night set for a Quiet Storm

Storm winds
Gently carries us across the night sky

The ease in the breeze
Brings a moment of tranquility
White clouds painted on a canvas
Of sky blue softens the mood
The mist in the air sprinkles us
We are blessed by Morning Light

We made it through the Quiet Storm

MY BEST POETRY
(The Best Part Of Me)

My best poetry is yet to come
Cause I know, JAH has a higher purpose
For me

Nineteen years I've toiled
Perfecting my style
Developing my gift of creativity
Mastering my craft
That I may share what GOD
Inspires in me

You see
You might just be the one
To get the best part of me
My heart, My Love, My Best Poetry

No matter how much I look back and think
How I could have done things differently
Or change certain things about me
I do believe, right now, where I am
Is where I'm supposed to be
I know who I am
Is who I'm supposed to be

Through the fire, I've been forged
Faced my trials and tribulations
I will always bear the cross
That was given to me

If my ink should run dry
And I never write another poem
Or verse another song
Know that there will always be a poem on my lips
And a song in my heart for you

When I have said all that, I had to say
When words begin to elude me
I will still have beautiful words to sing to you
You will always have the best part of me

SPECIAL REQUEST

I got a special request last night.
She said, hold me close,
Make me feel special tonight.

So, I wrapped myself around her,
Molding my body to her shape;
As she gently pressed her body
Against mine, I whispered these
Words in her ear:

I am the one who feels special tonight;
As you share your heaven with me,
On this full moon night.
There is nowhere else
On this earth, I would rather be,
Than laying right here behind you.

No feeling in this world could ever feel this good.
Holding you in my arms, your body heat warms me.
Right now, my soul is on fire,
Cause your sensuous scent is very pleasing to me.

To emancipate your intimate desires,
This is My Greatest Pleasure.
Now, I am honored to be the one,
You opened your heart to.

CHAPTER IX
RUDENESS OR HUMAN NATURE?
- For Mature Readers -

WHEN THE SUN SETS
(When The Sun Rises)

When The Sun Sets,
I Would Like To Find Myself Next To You;
Anticipate Sharing "One Moment,"
Becoming ONE With You.

As The Moment Draws Near
With Every Passing Hour,
The Night Blesses Our Intentions
With Peace And Tranquillity.

Bare And Exposed, We Embrace;
Our Hearts Beat In Sync,
Our Essence Blends,
We Melt Into Each Other.

As We Explore One Another,
Every Touch Heightens The Ecstasy.
Tender Kisses We Exchange,
From Head To Toe, Back And Front;
No Boundaries In Place.
We Are Free
To Touch And Kiss Wherever,
Experience The Joy Of
Giving Pleasure.

Ready To Experience
My Righteousness,
You Welcome My "One Black Love,"
I Enter With Compassion
And Sensitivity.
That You May Feel Every Inch
Of Every Stroke, I Take It Nice And Slow;
Long Or Short Shallow Or Deep,
I Keep My Rhythm Steady.

Up And Down In And Out,
Round And Round All About;
If I Stay Strong,
The Pleasure Will Last Long,
No Doubt.

As The Passion Increase,
I Feel The Release Of Your Warm
Succulence.
I Attempt To Holdback My River A Bit Longer,
That I May Take You
To Much Higher Levels Of Ecstasy.
My Mind And My Will Were Strong,
But My Flesh Was Weak;
With The Power Of The Nile River,
Unwillingly I Released...
As We Embrace Under The Stillness
Of The Moment, We Pray,
"IGZIABEHER!"

And When The Sun Rises,
I Would Like To Find Myself
Lying Next To You.
To Awaken To Your Radiant Sunshine;
To Begin The Day Anew,
But Never Forget Last Night
I Made Love To You.

MAKE LOVE TO YOU

I want to make love to you
Spiritually, physically and mentally

Yes, I want our spirits to mix, blend as ONE
I want You and I to share this highest form
Of intimate union
Where just being in your presence makes
My Nature rise, Strong!
And the amorous look in my eyes
Heightens your Ferine emotions

Spirit to spirit
Just focusing on our energy
The density of our aura, our essence
Forms a rainbow haze around us
In this place, only the spirit exist
This Is True Intimacy

Missionary, standing up
You on top or me hitting from the back
This is ferine, all about the physical
Bodies: drenched, soaked, saturated
Genitals: wet, drippin', soft, moist
Engorged, erect, hard, strong
You and I meeting stroke for stroke
Yes, just sex

Kissing, touching
Oral feasting
It's all about me tasting you
And you tasting me
Carnal pleasure, erotic desires
Sexual bliss

When we are so into each other
That we anticipate every move
The other makes
Just by the tone in your moan
I can hear your desires
Your intimate wants and needs
My eyes tell you how much
I've been longing
To truely give you all of me
"Your thoughts to my thoughts
My thoughts to yours
My mind to your mind
Your mind to mine."

I Will Always Love You!

NENA MOJADOS

Como una rosa
Floreciendo en algo bello
Nena abre para mi

Con matices de color
Oro latino a marrón ébano
Rojo hibisco mezclado con rosa dulce

Mi intención esta enfocada
Un lento viaje al éxtasis
Ese es el propósito
En este Rito Antiguo

Nena moja
De las suaves caricias
De la caricia sonora de mis dedos

Como lágrimas de alegría
Ella llora gotas blancas perla
Chorreando agua
Una reacción a mi
Entrega desinteresada de
Placer sincero

Dentro de sus paredes masajeo y acaricio
Con mi mas profunda sensibilidad
Revolviendo su calor y ardiendo
Su fuego

Llego profundo y acaricio su lugar sagrado
Nena se moja y se extasia en éxtasis

NENA WETS

Like a rose
Blooming into a thing of beauty
Nena opens for me

With shades of color
Latin gold to Ebony brown
Hibiscus red mixed with sweet pink

My intent is focused
A slow journey to ecstasy
That's the purpose
In this Ancient Rite

Nena Wets
From the gentle strokes
Of my fingers' probing caress

Like tears of joy
She cries pearl-white drops
Dripping wet
A reaction to my
Selfless giving of
Sincere pleasure

Inside her walls, I massage and caress
With my deepest Sensitivity
Stirring her heat and blazing
Her fire

I reach deep and caress her sacred spot
Nena wets and raptures in ecstasy

LONGING

Are You Longing
For Those Hot Summer Nights
When My Breath Whispers
Across Your Ears
Saying
I Want To Feel Your Love Tonight
To Feel The Heat
Of Your Sexual Desire
I Want My Love
To Flow Inside Of You
Keep My Rhythm
Steady And True

Come
Let Me Set
Your Thighs On Fire
Dip Into Your Sweetness
Lick Your Honey
From My Fingers
Let Me Taste
Your Sweet Black Flavor
Slurrrp
The Flavor Of
Your Black
Cherry's Juice

I Long To See
Your Eyes Role
Make Your Body Tremble
Feel Your Vagina Quake
Under The Power
Of My Long
Steady Strokes

Are You Longing

To Give It Up
From Behind
To Arch Deeper
Spread Wider
That You May Feel
My One Black Love
Stretching Far
Reaching Deep
Touching
Your Heart
Touching
Your Soul

Yea Babe
Let Me Enter
Your Velvet Gates
Passionately
Let Me
Stick It Up In The Air
Strong And Firm
Go Ahead Straddle
My Righteous Manhood
Let Me Feel The Caress
Of Your Velvet Walls
As You Glide
Up And Down
My Penis
I Know
You Are Longing
To Work It
Strong

Yea
I See It In Your Eyes
You Hunger
For That Rich Smoothness
Of My Deep Chocolate's

Milk
To Get To The Center
Of My Tootsie Roll
Pop
Slurp

Are You Longing
To Feel Me
Under The Stillness
Of The Night
For Me
To Cool The Fire
That Burns
Between Your Legs
As I Release My
Mighty River
As I Bless You
With My Liquid
Essence
I Can See
In Your Eyes
You Are Longing
For More

CHAPTER X
SHE SAID HE SAID
- Duets -

THE PERFECT STARTING PLACE

You really found my Message
In the Bottle, 'cause you knew
Just what to do.

Being with you was like time stopped
And nothing else existed, but Me and You
Kissing you was like leaving Earth
Ending up in Heaven.

With you, I tasted sweetness
From places I've never tasted sweetness before
You touched places I've never been touched
I tasted paradise with you.

When you held me in your arms
I was swept away to a place I never knew
A place I've never been before
You looked into my eyes and entered my heart
You went straight into my soul
There we found the perfect starting place.

Your body was perfect
Easy to hold and squeeze gently
But the best part is your acceptance of me
Just the way I am, all of me
You are loving, sweet, and kind
Someday real soon
I will make you all mine

You gave me the most perfect gift
Just by being you, and for that
I say, "I Love You"
Your Love made it very easy for me
With your gentle kisses & caresses
You had that special touch with me

161

The things I imagined about you
Didn't even come close to the realities of you
You are not just a dream come true
You are "My Dream Come True"

Lydia and David

BASK IN MY WORLD

Come Bask In My World
And join me as we experience wonderful things
New to You and Me

Let Us together find
That which, for so long, we have searched
Let us re-capture the simple times
We never knew together
Still looking ahead
To what this New World might hold

Let Us take One Moment
That One Night
And extend it another day
And another day, and another day
After that

Come Let Us Bask
In this New World, We create
Just for Us Two
Delighting in Each Others' presence
Let Us take pleasure
In Each Others' embrace
Squeezing gentle and tight

Will you come with me to Bask In Our World?

David

BASKING IN MY WORLD

I can make the violets open just for you every day at 10:00 am
To make September 4 every day the day you came from Heaven

I can make you wake each day with a sigh
Make your destiny my refuge, a day of Yours My Century
I can make the warmth of my soul keep you warm each winter
And in the summer have You drink sweet water from My well

I can make your walk in life be just like mine
Your laughter and your tears shared alike

I can make the stars light your nights
And paint the moon blue just for You
I can make the Heavens transfer to your door each day

I can make each drop of rain our embrace
And every sunshine a kiss of a different flavor

With My distinct color, texture, and taste
I can make My Love alone delight You

And all Your pleasures proof

Will you come with me to bask in My World?

Lydia

BETWEEN MAN AND WOMAN

Let us build a home together.
Join me, my African Knight
Because it is you, I do adore.
Time will tell
If the truth of you and I are forever.
It's not going to be easy,
Barriers will always be there
And so much more.

On a strong foundation
Let us make this commitment stand
My Queen, let us walk this road
Your hand in my hand
Our hands in GOD's
In truth, what the future holds
Is not known to us
But this you should know
I adore you too, my lady
Very much

A rare Essence of Pure Africa,
As Sunlight is from The Sun,
A Special quality you are.
Through divine guidance from Heaven,
Heal our minds with LOVE,
Heal the pains of Loss with Unity.

Come with me
Forward to the beginning
When I saw you, and you saw me
What brought us together
Pure True Righteous Love
Let us remember
GOD is our Center
GOD surrounds us

We encircle each other

My Knight, You rescued me from despair.
Look into my eyes, and fill my spirit.
Touch my hand, Love is nearby,
My Love is Yours, it's Ours.
We will join as one, anointed with Sweet Honey.

For I only exist
To be inside your spirit
To feel your touch deep within me
I exist only
To Love You
To give you all of me

You are my African Knight, My KING!
Leader, Lead my heart with Righteousness
And let us join minds.
I will listen, follow and work with you.
We can re-assemble this Universe with Love,
As in GOD's Plan, we are love,
Between a Man and a Woman.

Marilyn & David

CAN I

Can I Touch You There
Fingertips On Your Neck
Lips To Skin,
Moist With Desire
The Meeting Of Which
Ignites A Slow Burning Fire

Can I Kiss You Here
Taste The Sweetness
Of Your Heart
My Lips To Your Lips
Soft And Tender
Your Spirit To Mine
Keep This Slow Fire Burning
If Only For Just
One Moment In Time
Would You
Could You
Be Mine

Can I Touch You There
Hands On Your Thighs
A Gentle Circular Motion
And My Intent Is Clear
A Slow Journey To Ecstasy
Take Turns Guiding...
First Me
Then U
Then U
Then Me

Can I Hold You
Body To Body
Desires' Heat Rising
Easing Your Tension

Setting Your Emotions Free
Show Me Where
Let Me Take You
To Higher Ecstasy
Move Me To Your Pleasure,
The Center Of Your Soul
Show Me How
Whisper Your Deepest Desires In My Ear
Tell Me When
Can I Touch You There?
Can I?

Carmen & David

DUSTY ROAD

As I walk down this dusty road
I find memories of days long gone by
When I use to leave my dust in the wind
Dragging my feet, kicking stones
Walking ole dusty roads

Like leaving my footprints behind me
Walking ole dusty beaches
And kicking dusty sand

Collecting seashells
Pretending they were my treasure
Listening inside an empty conch shell
I could hear the ocean
I jumped the mighty waves
And didn't have a care

This dusty road I walk
Reminds me of the trees I never climbed
The fences I never jumped
The roads I never walked
The girls I never got to kiss

The butterflies I chased
The beautiful, lighted sky
The many stars I counted at night

I remember
The friends I grew up with
The many childhood games we played

Yes, this dusty road
Puts me in a peaceful meditative state
That I may reminisce on youthful days
And receive inspiration from THE MOST HIGH

OUR SPECIAL UNION

Just thought it'd be nice to duet with you
You are an inspiration to me
And we have so much in common, us two
We believe in God, have Cerebral Palsy
And share a few of the same hobbies

No doubt, it's a natural thing
Maybe pre-destined to happen
Your words and my words flowing
Entwined together, shows skill and artistry
But to a lost soul, they can be Light.
At the end of their dark tunnel

Another thing that comes to mind
We are a one of a kind
What I'm trying to say is
When I look at you, face to face
It's nice to see a brother of my own race
Nice to know someone other than God
Understands the struggles I have,
From day to, day

Where you are
Is where I have been
Where I am is where you're headed
But we can still learn from each other
Believe it or not, we are on the same journey
Maybe at different points, but we are here
For GOD'S Glory

It's a blessing to be given someone to go to
When you need an ear to hear you out,
Or an encouraging word sent your way
It's a blessing to be someone to come to
To hear a cheering word
170

And to be someone of experience
To call upon

Kia and David

SWEET POETRY TOGETHER

You say you don't have the talent
It's not in your blood
But I think different
Whether if it's the words we rhyme
The way we flow on paper
Or the way our bodies groove together
I do believe we can make
Sweet Poetry Together

Pen to paper
That's the way I flow
Just give me some time
And I'll have you Flowin' too
I express a creative word or phrase
Then you compliment with a verse or two
That's sweet poetry
Written by you and me

I know I have the talent
And yes, it's in my blood
But I just prefer
To read the flow on paper
With my mind in motion
Reading your antidotes
I do believe your words
Bring out the smile in me
Sweet Poetry

Words to mind, mind to visions
That's the way I perceive and listen
Just give me some time
Just keep your words flowin'
And I will keep reading
Expressing creative words
And expressing the meanings

172

Now that I have done a verse or two
Tell me what you think
The sweet poetry, written by you
Has done to me?

Maybe it's a part of your healing
Or that for which you have been longing
But for me, it's merely my duty
To share with the world
What GOD inspires in me

Angela & David

CHAPTER XI
SEASON'S END

CANDLE IN THE STORM

More than forty days and forty nights,
Like a candle in the storm, I stood.
Battered by the raging wind
Soaked by the drenching rain.

Yet,
No matter how heavy the smothered weight,
No matter how stifling the dense elements,
My flame would not go out,
My flame would not surrender.

You see,
GOD'S Loving Grace
Was A Shield around me.
Yes, JAH set HIS Angels
To watch over me.

Day and night, I stood alone
Dark and cold, my tears froze
As they flowed down my cheeks.
But, like a candle, on THE ROCK
I stood, amid the storm,
And My flame would not go out,
My flame would not surrender.

Yes!
JAH set HIS Angels
To watch over me.
GOD'S Loving Grace
Was A Mighty Shield
All Around me.

I weathered the storm,
Faced my trials and tribulations.
Many nights my tears ran like a river,

Many times my weeping endured
Through the night,
But my joy, my sweet joy
Has come with the morning light.

A Candle In The Storm,
My flame will not go out,
My flame will not surrender,
For JAH Loving Grace
Is A Mighty Shield
Around me;
JAH set HIS Angels
To watch over me.

MY POETESS

With the smooth flow of her pen,
She wrote her love on my heart;
Every verse was an expression from deep within,
Of how I made her soul sing.

Her heart desires unconditional love
With the freedom to spread her wings,
Cause she was born to fly.

Goodbye, My Poetess...

PURPLE

I can only imagine
How Purple looks on you
The way it complements
Your golden hue
Yes, purple and gold
Majestic colors and you

My fingers tingle, thinking about
How Purple feels on you
As it lays between my fingers and your skin
Silky and smooth
Purple passion
Me and You

I want to see
Purple on you
From head to toe
And every space in between
Purple on soft places
Purple on round places
Purple in between sweet spaces

179

OUR LOVE CHANGED

I was ready to love you
Forever Past Eternity
And set you, as my head
Cornerstone

Just The Way You Are
I wanted you, no conditions
Love doesn't need to understand
Love just needs "to love"

My Destiny Fulfilled
That's who I thought you were
My Island Breeze
I thought you were
My Rose Now

High Tide Low Tide
I stood by you
I gave you a place
To Let Your River Run
A place for you to release

Your love changed
So, I had to change my love too
Things are just not quite the same
As they use to be
I'm Still Diggin' You, this is true
But it's impossible to be in-love
With someone who's not in-love
With me.

I don't think that
The World Should Know
We are no longer together
Cause it will break their hearts

STILL DIGGIN' YOU

It's been a long time
Since I felt you
Your spirit moving inside me
The beat of your heart
Your rhythm I used to dance to

Just having sweet thoughts of you
Have been hard to come by lately
Your footsteps walking across my mind
Have become light, now I seldom see your face
Before I close my eyes at night

But,
I'm Still Diggin' You, Babe
Cause deep down, I know
We are meant to be
There's no way I'm going to lose
This upper hand
Someone else has to draw
That bad card

Three hundred and sixty-five days
Have long gone by
Since I put my lips to yours
My arms no longer remember
What it feels like to hold you
And my body has lost its mold
To the shape of you

Your picture next to my bed
Reminds me of the physical details of you
If I didn't have it, all I would have
Is a silhouette that resembles you

Despite all that has been said

I am Still Diggin' You
No doubt Babe, this is True
And I won't deny this Great Love
That I have for you

SEASON'S END

Some things last for a lifetime
Others last just for a season
But I do believe everything happens
For a reason

Seasons change
That's just the natural order of things
It doesn't matter how much we pray
For things to stay the same
Seasons will change

We may not have made it
To the pot of gold
But at least we got a chance
To smile at the rainbow

Our time lasted only for a season
Only JAH knows for what reason
But we crossed babylon's river together
Then were put asunder
JAH Will That Day.
SEASON'S END

But, like the sun
I'm ready to rise again
Shake lose my winter blues
And get ready for what spring
Brings anew

I am ready to end
My time of hibernation
Cause, as the cliché goes,
"Time waits for no one"
This is a lesson hard-learned

Love is in the air
I can smell it
Like rain, that's about to fall
Cool and fresh
And it's coming my way

I'm going to spread my arms
Lean back and point my face
To the sky
And let the rain pour down on me

Cause, as the cliché goes,
"Time waits for no one"
This is a lesson hard-learned

CHAPTER XII
I WROTE A SONG

MOVE IRIE
(song version)

<u>Chorus:</u>
Say You got to Move Irie
Live Up and Be Free
You got to Move Irie
Hail HIS MAJESTY
You know You got to Move Irie
Living Naturally
Move Irie
In Rastalivity

Awe remember that Bob Marley said
"Every man got a right to decide his
Own destiny"
So he can do what he wants
He may choose to abandon his divine responsibility
Or He may' Give a little More than he gets
Work a little harder than he sweats
Give a little More than he gets
Work a little harder than he sweats

Bingiman Move Irie
And greet Your bredren in passing:
Sometimes you gono to say, Roots Roots Root
Sometimes you gono to say, Yes I
Sometimes you gono to say, RasTafarI
Times we gono to say, Haile Selassie I
For every man should be, a bredren
Until we get to know him
Judge no man right or wrong
But live right and do right in JAH JAH Sight
Live right and do right, spread Your divine light

(CHORUS...)

Rastaman Move Irie
And Praise JAH in everything You do
Stretch forth Your hands in the morning and Praise H.I.M.
Lift up Your eyes at noontime and Praise H.I.M.
Humble Your head in the evening and Praise H.I.M.
Commune with Your Heart at bedtime and Praise H.I.M.
Youthman Move Irie
That Your days may be long
Sista Dread Move Irie
That Your days may be long

Really really and Truely
It's not for I to sey
Really really and Truely
It's not for De I to sey
Do Dis do dat
What is what's not
Do Dis and do dat
Or what is and what's not
But I man must look within I an I Life
Iman got to look within I an I Life
Anda Move Irie
Move Irie
Say, Move Irie
Move Irie

Say I gotto Move Irie
I got to Live Up and Be Free
I got to Move Irie
I got to Hail HIS MAJESTY
I know I got to Move Irie
Living Naturally
I got to Move Irie
Ina Rastalivity

Irie

188

BRING BACK THE OLD DAYS
(V.I. Flag Waiving)

Intro. Melody:

I.   I can remember when I was a Youth man
Everybody loved to party
And when we party, yes we party hearty
We got merry we were happy
But nowadays nobody wants to party
And live in unity and live in harmony
Cause when you jump up on somebody big toe
They want to fight you, pull trigger on you
CHORUS:
Bring Back the old days of jouvert morning
Pack in the streets everybody tramping
People rubbing up in the jam
People making flag with their hand
And a handkerchief waving in the air

II.   All the turmoil going on in my islands
My native islands, my Virgin islands
The St. Tomians them can't take the heartache
And the Crucians them belly can't take
All the killing and the victimizing and the Youth them
Daily they're dying

III.   The policeman them searching for solution
To this problem, this serious problem
We need unity and understanding
One Love, One Love
So everybody come and join with me
And sing this chorus in unity e e e
CHORUS:
Bring Back the old days of jouvert morning
I long to see even granny jamming
People jumpin up in the band

People making pole with their arms
And the V.I. flag waving in the air

We long for the old days of jouvert morning
Jam Band a keep everybody pumping
Woman rubbing up on their man
Woman making flag with their hand
And a handkerchief waving in the air

IV.   And now its time for us to come together
And show some real love to one another
Let us stretch forth our hands unto the FATHER
For HIS Salvation and HIS Guidance
Caribbean People lets all live as ONE
A divided nation can never stand
CHORUS:
Do you remember the old days of jouvert morning
Look up King Street to see a tramp coming
Man working up on woman
Man making pole with their arms
And the V.I. flag waving in the air

5/30/1996

DISTANT DRUMS
(Original Dub-poet version)

I n I hear de sound a De Drums
Trodding on de wind;
Sounding from Mount Zion,
Sounding from Mount Zion,
De Drums!
De Distant Drums, De Beating Drums,
Beating, sending, sending a message;
Afrika, Afrika, Afrika Unite!
Get Up Stan Up,
Stan Up fo Yo rights!
Drums, Drums beating fo Livity,
Beating fo Liberation,
Beating fo Inity;
Black Livity, Black Liberation, Black Inity.
De Drums!

Distant Drums, Ancient Drums;
Drums Telling, Telling I n I story,
Telling I n I Black-story.
Drums talkin bout Imhotep,
Hannibal, Akhenaton, Makeda,
Pianky, Cleopatra;
Drums talkin bout Zenobia, Nzinga,
Chaka, Chaka Zulu, Menelik I.
Drums, Talkin Drums, Drums sounding
From de bottom a de sea.
Drums dat speak de names of Billions
Of Afrikans who died traveling akras
De sea, on de journey into slavery.
Drums sounding from de bowels of de
Earth, speakin de names of Afrikans
Who died on de big, big plantations.
De Drums!

De sound a de Drums,
De Distant Drums,
Trods on de ocean waves;
Sounding, sounding from akras de ocean,
Sounding from De Lan of I n I Forfadas,
Alke-bu-lan, De Black Lan.
Distant Drums, sounding from akras de
Harba, sounding de call of
De Black Star Liner, ready fo departcha.
Sounding de call, Repatriation, Repatriation.
De Drums, De Callin Drums callin,
Callin You, callin Me,
Callin I n I n I, callin RasTafarI.
De Drums!

I n I hear De Distant Drums
Of De Prophets of Ancient Days.
De Drums of Isaiah sounding;
"Woe anto dem dat call evil good,
An good evil; dat put darkness fo
Light, an light fo darkness; dat put
Bitter fo sweet, an sweet fo bitter."
De Drums!

Yes, I n I hear De Distant Drums,
De Chantin Drums; De Bass Drums,
De Akette Drums, De Fundi Drums,
Niyabingi Drums. I man hear De Niyabingi
Drums Chantin; chantin babylon babylon
Yo trone gone dung, babylon yo
Trone gone dung.
Drums beatin fo over 400 years by
De rivers af babylon, Drums dat will
Never stop beatin until babylon walls Bun dung.
De Drums!

Listen, an I n I will hear De Drums;

De Distant Drums of Life, De Distant
Drums of Iration.
In de beginning was De Drums, an De
Drums was with JAH, an De Drums
Was JAH. An JAH played De Drums,
An JAH chanted; an whatsoIver JAH chanted,
WAS, an JAH saw dat IT was Irie.
De Drums!

Made in the USA
Monee, IL
30 July 2021